THE NEW
TURKEY

Directions for the 21st Century

Alan F. Scott

*For the people of the Republic of Turkey
who opened their arms and offered me a new life,
and for my family in New Zealand and Australia
who respected my choices, visit from time to time
and always make me welcome*

Contents

Preface to the First Volume

When I first came to Turkey in 1995, I knew little about the country. Well, that is not entirely true. As a New Zealander, I had grown up with the stories of the Gallipoli campaign, that bloody sideshow of the First World War, which cost so many lives and achieved so little. Brought up in a church-going family, I was well versed in the scriptures and gospels, especially the epistles of Paul to the churches of ancient Christendom. As a student of a model English grammar school, I spent five years studying Latin and the achievements and culture of the Roman Empire. Being a reader, and having an interest in history, I knew, of course, of the Byzantine and Ottoman Empires. I had even heard of Mustafa Kemal Atatürk, and somewhere or other had come across the modern Turkish alphabet, a deceptively familiar yet not-quite-accessible version of our Latin-based one, with its peculiar accent marks and unexpected cedillas. My studies of 19th century European history had familiarised me with 'The Eastern Question' and 'The Sick Man of Europe', and my readings of Shakespeare had mixed ominous references to the 'heathen Turk' with the folk culture that embodied names like Genghis and Attila with a power of evil beyond the capacity of mere words.

Yet I had no concept of the country that is the modern Republic of Turkey. I had all these snippets of knowledge buzzing around in what I liked to think of as my world-view. But I had no unifying idea that they all occurred within the boundaries of that little known and little understood nation on the back-doorstep of Europe.

Perhaps it was to my advantage that I came from a country far from the fast lanes of geopolitics. There was no visible Turkish diaspora in New Zealand to imbue me with a prejudice against migrant workers. My prejudices were more deep-seated and subliminal, but nonetheless real, being part of the cultural baggage I carried as an educated product of an Anglo/ Euro-centric system and culture.

Almost from the moment the wheels of my British Airways Boeing hit the tarmac at Atatürk Airport, I found these cultural assumptions challenged in ways that I had never imagined. In the years since then, while making a life for myself as a teacher of English in Turkey, I have continued to benefit from the mind-expanding shocks and jolts that strike the foreigner in this much-misunderstood land.

I remember looking at an atlas, on first coming to Turkey. It was quite a good atlas, a reputable publication that I had bought while studying Geography at Auckland University. I still have it, in fact, and I have counted twenty-one pages on the British Isles, ten pages on the United States of America, and even little old New Zealand warrants a two-page spread. Interestingly, however, there is not one single page devoted to the modern Republic of Turkey, a country three times the size of New Zealand, or Great Britain, or Japan, and in population, second only to the united Germany among European nations.

It is a small thing, perhaps, and of no special significance. I've never been a fan of conspiracy theories. But again, I couldn't help being puzzled when I learnt that the Turks celebrate 18 March as Victory Day in their Çanakkale War (which we know as the Gallipoli campaign). Hang on a minute! We (Anzacs etc) didn't even get there till 25 April! As educated adults, we need to feel confident that history has an objectivity that places it above partisan politics and racial stereotypes, so how to account for this major disparity of dates? In fact, as I later learned, the Gallipoli landings were Plan B, made necessary because of the failure of Plan A. For the Turks, their success in turning back the Royal Navy from the Dardanelles was the more important part of the victory. For the British Empire, no doubt, that was a setback better consigned to the footnotes of history.

Historical events, dates and personages are one aspect of the construct of the world that we all carry with us. But there is another, less overt, perhaps more powerful force shaping our judgments of other peoples and races: the proverbial wisdom, folk knowledge and cultural assumptions that we inhale with the air of the society in which we grow up and receive our education. So Genghis Khan and Attila the Hun have such a basic existence in the consciousness of Western minds that no knowledge of history is necessary to conjure up images of marauding barbaric hordes sweeping out of the Asian steppe, laying waste all in their path like an invasion of killer bees. When I learned that the principal of my school, a tall, distinguished-looking gentleman of scholarly bearing was called Genghis, it required in me a shift of mental gears. Hearing also that Attila was the name of that polite, hand-raising, homework-doing young lad in my year 9 class was a further surprise for which my Euro-centric upbringing had not prepared me.

I would like to share some of the experiences I have had since I first came to this surprising country, and some of the eye-opening knowledge that has come my way, bringing me to a better understanding of a place that has become my second home.

Alan Scott
Istanbul
April 2011

Preface to the Second Volume

Two years have passed since the first edition of 'Turkey File' went to press, and much has happened in Turkey and the world in that time. Some of that book's contents are historical and retain their relevance, while others have been overtaken by recent events.

For better or worse – though mostly, I believe, for better - a new Turkey is taking shape. The democratisation process has gathered momentum, while at the same time, cracks have started to appear in the coalition of interests brought together under the banner of the Justice and Development Party. The Middle East continues to play a major role in international affairs. New alliances are formed while armed struggles and old enmities seethe above or beneath the surface.

The so-called 'Arab Spring' produced revolutionary changes in some countries in the region, but on the whole, outcomes have probably been disappointing – at least to those who hoped for a brave new world of democracy and respect for human rights. Egypt's flirtation with open elections was short-lived and a military coup more or less restored the earlier status quo. Syria's President Bashar al-Assad steadfastly refuses to step down in the face of increasing bloodshed. Violence and lawlessness continue in Libya and Iraq despite the demise of Muammar Gaddafi and Saddam Hussein.

In the meanwhile, the government of Israel continues to defy majority international opinion in its probably vain search for permanent acceptance and security. Saudi Arabia and other oil rich states continue building monuments to Mammon behind a veil of spirituality. One positive note may have been sounded by the nuclear deal brokered between the United States and Iran – but time alone will tell.

Amidst these events, Turkey remains an island of relative peace, stability and democracy. Of course, located as it is on the doorstep of the Middle East, with its majority Muslim population, its government is obliged to steer a careful course between the oil-thirst and control freak-uency of Western nations, and its insecure and unstable neighbours to the east. At the same time, its location at the back door of Europe, its religious demographics and its colourful history stand in the way of acceptance into the Western world of developed nations which it so strongly desires.

All these issues influence the way the citizens of Turkey see themselves, and the way they are seen by outsiders. In addition, there are the internal complexities of forging an identity from the mixture of races, religions and cultures that have passed over this bridge between east and west for millennia, leaving their footprints on the land and its people. Modern Turkey has inherited so much of the archeological wealth of civilisations Western society likes to think of as its own forebears – yet its 'otherness' in relation to that Western society has brought a good deal of misunderstanding, criticism and resentment.

This new collection of essays explores some of the events and issues that affect the modern Republic of Turkey and its place in the world. There is a new dynamism evident to all, affecting every facet of life in the country. As with all periods of rapid change, people are unsettled, and there is friction. In the end, I believe, the social upheavals taking place in Turkey were inevitable and essential. I am confident that a stronger and healthier society will emerge, and I hope my optimism comes through in the pages that follow.

Alan Scott
Istanbul
December 2013

Turkey's Historical Heritage - Drop a spade into the ground

22 July 2011

Gümüşlük, on the Bodrum peninsula of Turkey's south Aegean Coast, is our getaway retreat of choice for the hot summer months. My morning routine is to cycle four or five kilometres to the village bakery to get simits for breakfast. In case you didn't know, simits are one of the reasons people choose to live in Turkey – and one of the things Turks miss most when they are away from home. A simit is a bagel-shaped bread roll, whose crispy crust is coated with sesame seeds, the perfect accompaniment for a Turkish breakfast of feta cheese, honey, olives, sliced tomatoes and cucumbers.

Cycling as a post-modern lifestyle choice is still not a big thing in Turkey, and a guy of my age sweating and grunting around country roads is something of a curiosity. I used to greet the sentry at the gate of the local gendarmerie, and we would exchange a brief word of mutual appreciation for the demanding tasks we were undertaking . . . until this year. Now there is no sentry, and the white double-storey building that used to house him and his military colleagues stands empty. The Bodrum peninsula is an Aegean paradise of white stucco houses, crimson bougainvillea, azure sea and never-ending sunshine . . . but there is, of course, a downside. Currently, our household water is trucked in and rationed out from a central reservoir at certain hours of the day. We, and most of our neighbours, have circumvented this inconvenience by installing our own tank with a pump that allows us the luxury of a 24/7 water supply. Now, however, in response to demand, the local council is working on a pipeline that will connect us to the town water supply system, and herein, in case I had left you wondering, can be found the reason for the disappearing gendarmes. But before I solve that mystery for you, I want to digress a little into the mists of prehistory.

There was an exhibition recently at the Sabancı Museum in Istanbul, entitled, simply, *'Across'* (*'Karşıdan Karşıya'* in Turkish). The exhibition contained artifacts from the civilisation that existed in the Cycladic Islands around 3000 BCE. These people, among the first to turn pottery on a wheel and smelt metal for tools and weapons, interacted and cross-fertilised with similar groups on the south Aegean coast of Anatolia, where lies our little village of Gümüşlük. Its geographical advantages have long been recognised, among them, a natural harbour with a circular bay almost enclosed by a narrow peninsula sheltering it from the prevailing winds. Today, tourists are given sketchy information about the ancient city of *Myndos* that grew around the shores of this bay. Indeed, the observant visitor will notice finely dressed black stones reused in modern buildings, fragments of marble columns lying in the fields, and door posts and architraves, clearly from an earlier time, garnishing the deconsecrated village church.

Like many ancient sites in Turkey, Myndos has yet to be excavated by archaeologists, and surprisingly little is known about its history. However, excavations of another kind are currently progressing, with the aim of laying the pipeline that will carry the town water supply I mentioned earlier. Apparently, workmen tunnelling beneath the gendarme base near Gümüşlük stumbled upon the remains of an ancient necropolis. Luckily for historians and archaeologists, there was at least one person in the construction crew capable of recognising the find for what it was, and the gendarmes have had to move their operations to an empty school building in the vicinity.

Who knows what will come to light once experts start to uncover the long-hidden secrets of Myndos? Ancient Greek writers attributed the origins of the city to the Leleges, generally assumed to have been the aboriginal inhabitants of Anatolia. When Alexander the Great arrived on the scene in 334 BCE, it was part of the kingdom of Caria, owing allegiance to the Persian Empire. The capital of this kingdom was Halicarnassus (modern Bodrum), famous for the wondrous funerary edifice erected by Queen Artemisia on the death of her brother (and husband) King Mausolus, from whose name we derive our word *mausoleum*. That was nearly two-and-a-half millennia ago, and the site has been continuously inhabited since, passing from Hellenic hands, through classical Roman, Byzantine and Ottoman to modern times. The church I mentioned earlier, lost its primary purpose after the population exchanges following the Turkish War of Independence in the 1920s. These days it comes to life again in the summer months when it hosts well-attended concerts of classical music.

By now you have probably guessed the reason for the title of this piece. If you drop a spade into the ground pretty much anywhere in modern Turkey, you stand a good chance of unearthing astounding evidence of an earlier civilisation. I feel sorry for Turkish school kids for many reasons – but one in particular is the amount of history they have to learn. If you, like me, struggled with the Tudors and Stuarts, the causes and course of the Hundred Years War, or the incomprehensible entities historians refer to as the Holy Roman and Hapsburg Empires, spare a tear of sympathy for the Turkish child, required to come to grips with a mind-numbing assortment of sequential and overlapping societies and civilisations extending back to Palaeolithic times.

The Museum of Ancient Anatolian Civilisations in Ankara recognises the need for ten further sections after the Neolithic Age ended in Anatolia around 5500 BCE. The Çatalhöyük site near Konya is recognised as one of the earliest urban conglomerations. Then follow:

- The Chalcolithic (copper/stone) Age (5500-3000 BCE), eg Alacahöyük.

- The Early Bronze Age (3000-1950 BCE), dominated by the Hatti tribes.

- Assyrian Trade Colonies (1950-1750 BCE), such as Kanesh Karum/Kültepe near the modern city of Kayseri

- Hittite Period (1750-1200 BCE), whose capital was Hattusa (modern Boğazköy).

- Phrygian Period (1200-700 BC), which produced the legendary King Midas.

- Late Hittite Period (1200-700 BC), whose best-known site is Carcemish.

- Urartian Period (1200-600 BCE), with sites in Eastern Anatolia, especially around Lake Van.

- Lydian Period (1200-600BCE), with another famous king, Croesus (the rich one).

- The Classical Period.

If that list is not enough to addle your brain, consider that the Carians and the Leleges are merely subsets, and the Classical Period, which lasted around a thousand years, encompasses all of Ancient Greek and Roman times. Then you have the Byzantines, generally considered to have had an Early, Middle and Late period in their own thousand-year history. Somewhere in that Late period, the Turks appeared on the scene and proceeded to establish two major empires, the Seljuks and the Ottomans, not to mention a confusing array of *beyliks* and fiefdoms.

In recent years, quite a number of spades have been dropped into the ground in Istanbul as a result of the Marmaray excavations. 'Marmaray' is a massive rail transit project aimed at linking the European and Asian sides of the city via a submarine tube under the Bosporus Straits. Several huge underground stations on the opposite shores will feed passengers into a network of lines fanning out all over the metropolis. The project was originally scheduled for completion around 2008 – but the first stage actually opened in 2013. 'Why?' you may ask. Are Turks really that disorganised and inefficient? The fact is that construction work has been constantly interrupted by the need to allow teams of archaeologists into the excavations to sift through the latest stupendous find.

Just to put this business in some kind of context, I would like to share with you brief excerpts from two books I came across recently. The first is entitled *'The World Beneath Istanbul'* by Ersin Kalkan[1]. It's not awfully well written (at least the English version), and is rather anecdotal than scholarly. However, it does open a fascinating subject. In his introduction, the author quotes Dr Johannes Cramer, of Berlin Technical University's Institute of Architecture: *'Did you know,'* he asks rhetorically, *'that the underground city of Istanbul is eight times bigger than that of Rome?'* I didn't, and I don't know how he arrived at that figure, but even allowing for some exaggeration and a generous margin for error, it's food for thought, isn't it! The second book is *'Walking Through Byzantium'* by Jan Kostenec[2], If you can't find the book, the website[3] is definitely worth a peek. Here's what Kostenec has to say in his introduction: *'Unlike other ancient capitals, modern Istanbul has witnessed virtually no urban archaeology, and basic elements of the Byzantine city, such as the street system, public spaces, and housing, remain all but unknown.'*

So, you can imagine hordes of drooling archaeologists lurking around the various Marmaray construction sites, trowels and wheelbarrows at the

---

1 Istanbul Büyükşehir Belediyesi, 2010

2 Grofbas, 2008

3 http://www.byzantium1200.com/

ready, waiting for the first glimpse of a marble fragment or a shard of pottery. As it turned out, the finds have been rather more spectacular, and provided sufficient material for an earlier exhibition at Sabancı Museum, entitled *'8000 Years of a Capital'*. In fact, finds dating back to 6000 BCE have considerably extended the time frame in which the site of Istanbul is known to have been continuously inhabited. Discoveries from more recent times include remains of the original city wall built by Constantine the Great in 330 CE, and the main harbour of the city he founded, the 4th century Port of Theodosius. The most spectacular find to date has been an almost intact medieval Byzantine galley, complete with all its cargo of amphorae and other goods.

The Marmaray project, clearly, has provided a rare opportunity for archaeologists to delve beneath the surface of the modern city of Istanbul. At the same time, it provides an illustration of the tension between the existence of a living city, and of the layers of history that lie beneath it. There can be few places on earth where this pressure is as great as in Istanbul, where the history is as long, and the pace of metropolitan growth so rapid.

A lesser-known example is the 9th century Christian Satyros Monastery[4] recently unearthed at Küçükyalı on the Asian side of the city. Küçükyalı is well within the urban sprawl of modern Istanbul, with its estimated population of fifteen million – but perhaps twenty kilometres beyond the walls of medieval Constantinople. Needless to say, excavations have necessitated some disruption to the local community, including the removal of a section of asphalt road and a children's playground, and have so far brought to light the large central monastery building and a water cistern with associated pipes and channels.

What we learn from this is that the archaeological riches of Turkey are not confined to contemporary population centres or sites mentioned in the visitors' guides. Anywhere in the country, an unsuspecting spade may suddenly turn up a Bronze Age figurine, a Roman villa or a Greek theatre. In fact, for my last example, I want to take you to a small city in the western

---

4 http://www.en.istanbul2010.org/proje/GP_584603

Black Sea region of Turkey. Zonguldak is a very new city by Turkish standards, having been founded in 1849 as the port for shipping coal from the mines of Ereğli. Nizamettin Oral, a 65 year-old farmer living in a nearby village, was excavating in his garden with the aim of building a greenhouse. What he found was the mosaic floor of a 3rd century Roman villa, which has led to two years of work by archaeologists from Ereğli Museum. More mosaics and frescos have been unearthed, and it has been suggested that the finds are part of a larger classical Roman settlement.

I haven't been able to learn what has happened to Nizamettin Bey, his farm, and the progress on his greenhouse. I would guess that agricultural activities have pretty much ceased in the vicinity. I hope that he has been well compensated by the government as an incentive to other citizens who may stumble upon similar discoveries. Clearly, another message that comes out of all this is that preserving the past is an expensive business – and for a country like Turkey, with an embarrassment of historical riches and an economy struggling to join the developed world, the money is not always easy to find. Imagine the cost overrun of that Marmaray project and its five-year delay! The 16th century Süleymaniye Mosque, flagship achievement of Ottoman master architect Sinan, was recently renovated at a cost of nearly $US 15 million.

In London, I remember seeing a small section of the ancient city wall in a glassed-off area of the Barbican Centre. I understand that other similar sections can be seen elsewhere by determined explorers. In Istanbul I have actually walked around the walls of the ancient city of Constantinopolis. It's relatively easy, in the sense that most of them are still standing – but difficult in another way. They are approximately twenty-two kilometres in circumference, and it took me three trips on separate days to complete the circuit. Restoration work is in progress. But at least they're above ground, and you won't need a spade to find them.

2

Returning the Treasures of Turkey - Credit Where Credit's Due

14 August 2011

One of the things I love about the *'blogspot'* site[5] is the statistics page. I check it obsessively at least twice a day to see who's reading me, what country you live in, and which of my posts attracted the most attention. Interestingly, a page which consistently receives many visits is one I wrote more than three years ago, entitled *'Where are the Ancient Treasures of Turkey?'* Well, I was very new to the blogging business in those days. In my attempts to create an identity, and to be provocative, some of my implied criticisms may have been a little unfair. It has been suggested to me that modern nations with ancient treasures weren't looking after them properly – and anyway, the governments of those nations gave permission to foreign archaeologists to carry off their finds.

Those claims may in fact be true, and I don't intend to examine them here. What I do want to do is bring to your attention, in case you may have missed them, three recent instances where a major museum in a

5 This book is based on articles written for the author's blog: www.turkeyfile.blogspot.com

western country has decided to return an important artifact to its place of origin.

Some years ago I visited the Egyptian Museum in Cairo. It was a marvellous experience, to see those fabled statues and relics of ancient Egypt that I was so familiar with from pictures and films. There was the eleven-kilogram solid gold mask of Tutankhamen sitting in a glass case. More interesting, though, for me, was a statue representing a gentleman by the name of Seneb, with his wife and children. This Seneb was, apparently, head of the royal weaving factories in the Sixth Dynasty (around 2200 BCE), and he was a dwarf. His wife, however, wasn't.

Perhaps you haven't had an opportunity to visit Cairo, but you may have done the next best thing, and toured the Egyptian section of the British Museum, which is also pretty impressive. I haven't actually been able to establish which of the two museums houses the greater number of mummies – but my impression was that the prize might go to the institution in London. Now it may be, as my critics suggest, that these mummies were all legally obtained, and anyway, they were just rotting away back there in Egypt. Nevertheless, I was heartened to read, in a *New York Times* article[6] that the Metropolitan Museum in New York has decided to take a lead in returning some disputed artifacts to their place of origin.

The British archaeologist Howard Carter discovered the tomb of Tutankhamen in 1922. Most of his major finds can be seen in the Cairo Museum, but it seems he did retain a number of nice pieces for his own private collection. On his death, these were bequeathed to the Metropolitan Museum which, at the time, maintained an *'expedition house'* in Egypt. When this was closed in 1948, the pieces were, it seems, *'transferred'* to the New York location. Discussions have, according to the report, been continuing for some time, but in July, the director of the 'Met' announced that nineteen artifacts, including a miniature bronze dog and a sphinx-shaped bracelet ornament, would be sent back to Egypt.

---

6 http://www.nytimes.com/2010/11/10/arts/design/10met.html

Well, pretty much everyone knows something about Ancient Egypt, the Pharaoh Tut and Howard Carter. It's a high profile case, and not altogether surprising that the dispute received international media attention. Less well known are similar disputes between the government of Turkey, and other renowned museums holding priceless antiquities found within Turkey's borders. Just a week before the Met's gesture, the Museum of Fine Arts in Boston announced that it would return the top half of a statue known as the *'Weary Herakles'*. Apparently the MFA had bought the piece in 1982 without thoroughly checking its provenance. Turkish authorities had finally convinced them that it was a perfect match for the lower half unearthed in Perge in Southern Turkey in 1980 – not so difficult given that the two halves of the statue were broken cleanly on a diagonal line.

Two months prior to this, the Prussian Cultural Foundation agreed to return a 3000-year-old Hittite sphinx. The sphinx was found by German archaeologists excavating the Hittite capital of Hattusha in 1907, and had been in the Pergamon Museum in Berlin since 1934. It was one of a pair of sphinxes forming part of the gate of Hattusha, dating from the 2nd millennium BCE, and will now be reunited with its mate in the Istanbul Archaeology Museum.

It's a vexed question whether antiquities are better left in situ or taken away for safekeeping. Few would argue that irreplaceable relics of ancient civilizations should not be taken to museums where they can be restored and preserved by experts. Further, not everyone has the opportunity to travel to distant parts of the world to see the original locations, so it is undoubtedly desirable that exhibitions of relics should be presented elsewhere. It is also true that not all nations are equally interested in preserving their historical and cultural heritage. The Buddhas of Bamiyan received international coverage when the Taliban government of Afghanistan dynamited them in March 2001. The missing genitals and breasts of classical Greek and Roman statuary are more a result of the prudishness of early Christians than the ravages of time. Similarly, the picturesque ruins of monasteries and abbeys dotted around the English landscape have been that way since Henry VIII, in his reformist zeal, decided to 'dissolve' them.

However, these days, most civilized countries recognize the need to restore and preserve their antiquities, and to build modern museums in which to house them. Museums and art galleries all over the world are part of a community that organize sharing and exchange of relics, artifacts and works of art for local exhibitions that are well publicized and well attended. It is undoubtedly best that five Caryatids on the porch of the Erechtheion at the Acropolis in Athens should be plaster copies, and the real ones displayed in the Athens Museum. More debatable is whether the British Museum itself might make do with a plaster copy, and return the sixth one to its true home.

Anyway, hats off to the Americans and the Germans for making a start!

3

UK Riots and the Istanbul Grand Prix - The End of the Golden Rapture?

25 August 2011

Faith and belief are marvellous things, aren't they? I've never been one for millenarianism or doomsday predictions. I never doubted for a moment that my Apple Mac would see me through to the 21st century. I'm content to meet my Maker when He (or She) decides the time has come, and I'd sooner not know the date in advance, though I can see how some might want to. I don't have a great deal of faith in politicians – but I do have some sympathy for the impossible situations democracy puts them in. They have to promise heaven and earth to get elected, then have to back-pedal rapidly when post-election reality bites. Hands up who really thought Barack Obama would be allowed to close Guantanamo and stop the water-boarding.

So I'm not generally one to point the finger at politicians and accuse them of breaking promises. I was pretty sceptical in the first place. And I'm certainly not generally given to laughing at the misfortunes of others.

Those recent riots in cities across the UK looked pretty scary, and nothing can excuse the burning of property and looting of businesses large or small. David Cameron's government re-established the rule of law, and good on him, you have to say. However, I couldn't help noticing that he pre-empted criticism by referring to his own pre-election promise to mend Britain's *'broken society'*. It seems that *'There are pockets of . . . society that are not just broken but frankly sick'* which seemed to suggest that mending society might be just a tad trickier than British voters had been led to believe. We need a medical professional rather than a simple repairman. But then most of us knew that already, right?

I'm not going to join the ranks of those who suggest that inequalities of wealth distribution are the root cause of these riots, and other forms of violent social unrest. I certainly do not intend to suggest that burning and looting are understandable or acceptable responses to social injustice. In fact, I want to agree one hundred percent with Dave Cameron in his belief that pockets of modern society are sick. On the other hand, I'm not sure he and I would agree totally on which *'pockets'*.

My work-place is located on the southern outskirts of Istanbul, on the Asian side of the city. It's a pleasantly green spot still, despite the building of airports, industrial complexes, monstrous shopping centres and acres of two-storey villas with private swimming pools. A kilometre or so across the fields from our campus stands Istanbul Park, venue for the Turkish Formula One Grand Prix. Most of the time it sits there, in patient torpor, waiting for the one weekend a year when it will spring to life, and the hills will echo to the whine of high performance engines operating at rpms that would cause our Honda Jazz to melt down to a blob of metal and plastic.

I couldn't help wondering what sort of money went into this project, so I checked it out, and I can tell you that Istanbul Park was built in 2005 at a cost of €80 million (about 200 million Turkish Liras at today's rates). I went to the Grand Prix in Auckland once. We didn't see any spectacular crashes, and we weren't sitting in a corporate box being served chilled Dom Perignon and crab claws, so maybe I didn't get the full effect, but honestly, I couldn't see what all the fuss was about. Still, I'm not one to spoil other people's fun. Sadly for those other people, however, it seems that the 2011 Turkish Grand Prix may actually be the last one to take place at Istanbul Park. Apparently Bernie Ecclestone, head honcho of international Formula One racing, decided to double the fees Turkey would be charged for hosting the race. The Turks said *'%&$#?@ off!'* or words to that effect, and that, it seems, is that.

Well, of course, running a business like Formula One racing costs money, and no one would begrudge Bernie his right to make a living – but this spat did come to mind when I saw a news item in July that the most expensive house in the USA had just been sold to . . . Bernie's 22-year-old daughter Petra. Reports say the 5,600 m² house in Bel Air, Los Angeles had been on the market for two years for $150 million, but some tough negotiating got the sellers down to $85 million. I just hope Petra's making a generous donation to help those starving kids in Somalia. By the way, for the sake of comparison, I read that Mr and Mrs Brad Pitt have just put their California mansion on the market for a relatively modest $13.75 million. I guess at that level, the 0.75 is still important.

Nevertheless, one swallow doesn't make a summer – and one sick billionaire doesn't make a sick society, right? But did you see that film, *'Inside Job'* that won the 2010 Oscar for best documentary? As the *Time* reviewers said: *'If you're not enraged by the end of the movie, you weren't paying attention.'* I've read a number of articles about a gentleman by the name of Stephen Schwarzman, CEO of the Blackstone Group. Most sources agree that he is a major player in the world of finance, and he has been quoted as saying in a speech in March 2009, that forty-five percent of the world's wealth had been destroyed by the global credit crisis. However, he took heart that the US government was committed to the preservation of financial institutions (like his, one assumes) and would do whatever it took to restart the economy. It's hard to establish exactly how much money Mr Schwarzman earns. Some sources say he made $5.1 billion in 2007, down to $702.4 million in 2008. Some say he took a ninety-nine percent pay cut in 2009 down to a paltry $350,000. Whatever the truth of it, it's a fair bet that a good chunk of that missing wealth ended up in his pocket.

But somehow, I suspect that's not one of the *'pockets'* David Cameron was referring to.

Getting back to Petra Ecclestone, and her generosity to the kids in Somalia, don't you find it interesting how a girl (or a guy) can make mega-tanker-loads of money from some dodgy enterprise, then, at some later date, donate large sums to a pet charity, and suddenly she's on the fast track to benefactor's heaven? Back in 1992 a Hungarian born gentleman of Jewish parentage by the name of George Soros achieved fame (or notoriety) as *'the Man who broke the Bank of England.'* Surprisingly, the 'breakage' didn't involve safe-cracking, ripping ATM machines from walls, armed holdups, or, in fact, any violence at all. The technique is known in the trade as 'short-selling', and, according to well-informed sources, it allowed George to pocket a cool $1.1 billion (whatever that was in sterling at the time).

Well, *Wikipedia* tells me that Mr Soros is *'a financier, businessman and notable philanthropist focused on supporting liberal ideals and causes'*, but it hasn't always been so. Back in 1997, when Asian economies suddenly began to crash, the Malaysian Prime Minister, Mahathir bin Mohammad, went public with his opinion that the crash of Asian currencies had in fact been caused by Mr Soros and his short-selling ilk. To be fair, it seems George didn't actually invent this dubious financial activity. That honour goes to a Dutch merchant named Isaac le Maire, who, it seems, came up with the scheme in 1609. Subsequently, the British Government banned it totally in the 18th century, but more recently un-banned it. Some economists blame short-sellers for the Wall Street Crash of 1929, and the US Government passed regulations controlling it – which, apparently, were also repealed in July 2007. Any significance in that date, I wonder? Still, you can't blame a guy for making a buck any way he can – but again, I feel pretty sure that Dave Cameron wasn't referring to George Soros's pockets when he sought the cause of the UK riots. Interestingly, one of united Europe's attempts to save their common currency has recently involved the banning of short-selling in Belgium, France, Italy and Spain.

If you don't live in the Southern Hemisphere, you probably don't care overmuch, but New Zealand hosted the Rugby World Cup Tournament in 2011. Old guys like me can actually remember when rugby was still an amateur sport, but these days, it sure as hell isn't. Professionalism, as you know, means a whole lot more than merely paying the players to play. Commercial sponsors are the life-blood of professional sport – but there are times when they seem to lose sight of the fact that, without the nameless millions of supporters, blood wouldn't flow. Sportswear giant *Adidas* is one of the major sponsors of the Rugby World Cup, and they upset rugby fans in New Zealand by offering to sell replica 'All Black' uniform jerseys for $NZ 220. Quite steep, you might think, especially with the strength of the NZ dollar – and most NZ rugby fans thought so too, more so when they found the jerseys were available online for about half the price . . . until, that is, *Adidas* managed to close the sites to purchasers in New Zealand.

Still, manufacturers are entitled to earn a fair living too, and, as the *Adidas* people pointed out, they invest a good deal of money in New Zealand rugby. On the other hand, most *Adidas* products are produced in Asian factories where workers typically earn around $1 an hour. It's been estimated that the cost of producing the replica All Black jerseys in a Chinese factory is approximately $8 – which left a tidy profit for the owners and shareholders of *Adidas* to pocket. But I don't suppose David Cameron was referring to those *'pockets'* either.

Back when I was a lad, science fiction was a popular literary genre. There were some prophets of doom, but, on the whole, there was a strong feeling around in those days that science had, or would soon have, the answers to most of the world's problems. Labour-saving devices would remove the drudgery from human existence, the green revolution would do away with famine and starvation, and anyway, if by chance we weren't able to solve all the problems on earth, such as over-population, it wouldn't be long before we set up colonies on the Moon, Mars, or other extra-terrestrial real estate. The future was generally expected to be Utopian.

Well, somehow, it doesn't seem to have worked out that way. A recent *Time* magazine article[7] on rapidly increasing global food prices suggests that the only way for prices from here is further up. Increasing population, climate change, the channelling of food-growing land to bio-fuel production and falling water tables will all contribute to a continuing rise of demand over supply. *'Enjoy your dinner tonight,'* the writer concludes. *'While you can still afford it.'*

So it seems that technology isn't going to save us after all, and you'd have to think that most of the major techno-companies in the world have figured that out. Make your buck while you still can, they seem to have decided. Get cell phones into the hands of the Somalian public, and at least they'll be able to keep in touch while they're dying of starvation. I guess it'll be a while before they can afford self-driving cars, but the rest of us have that to look forward to – once the automobile industry gets the bugs ironed out. Despite the entry of *Google* into the market, I'm backing the Germans to sort out that technology first. Apparently *Google's* self-drivers are still tail-ending each other on the testing circuit.

Well, if technology hasn't got the answers after all, what's a person to do? Surely there must be hope somewhere. Luckily, there is, and, according to another recent *Time* article[8], a lady by the name of Michele Bachmann has the matter in hand. Michele has stormed on to the scene as the possible Republican nominee to contest the US Presidency, and she's hot! Apparently God Himself thinks so, because, so she says, *'She's hot for Jesus Christ.'* This divine support has clearly struck a chord with Middle America – probably some of those recently disappointed by the failed doomsday predictions of Harold Camping. The *Time* writer quotes one of Ms Bachmann's supporters, a certain Becky Magee, as saying, *'I think Jesus is coming to get us. I think we'll be raptured soon.'*

Now I'm going to make a confession here, and confide in you that, until May 22, the day after Harold Camping and his flock attracted media

---

7 *Time,* July 25, 2011

8 *ibid.*

attention because the world didn't end as they had expected, I had always thought rapture had something to do with sex, drugs and rock'n'roll. But the world has changed in many ways, and even my *MS Word* dictionary hasn't caught up with the new usage, as evidenced by the squiggly red line underneath the word when I typed it. *Microsoft's* best suggestion was, in fact 'ruptured', which may not be far from the truth. My trusty old *Chambers* lexicon at least provided a range of options:

Rapture: *a seizing and carrying away* [it says], *extreme delight, transport, ecstasy, a paroxysm (a fit of extreme pain, laughter, passion, coughing, etc)*
 From Latin – to seize and carry off[9]

Well, much as I'd like to think Jesus or some other omnipotent immortal would come and save the world from the consequences of our greed and stupidity, I just can't seem to get my head around the concept. I have to say, it seems more likely to me that we've had the 'Rapture'; the good old days are over, and we'd better start figuring out ways to save ourselves and Planet Earth, because time, I reckon, is running out.

---

9 *Chambers English Dictionary*, 1990)

4

Cyprus, Turkey and the EU -
Getting it wrong again?

24 September 2011

I don't remember when I took out my first subscription to *Time Magazine*. I'm sure I must be one of their most loyal long-standing followers. Certainly there are occasions, generally during the lead-up to another United States presidential election, particularly when the opposition are going through the seemingly endless mumbo-jumbo of trying to select a candidate to challenge the incumbent, when I wonder why I bother. But I renew my subscription, mainly because I have never found a satisfactory substitute: a convenient and colourful package which keeps me more or less up-to-date with what's going on in the world, from arts and literature to technology and politics, international affairs, sport and economics, to medicine and the environment.

Sometimes you have to read between the lines, of course, and always be aware of its Americo-centric viewpoint – but lately they seem to have been working on that. I've been pleasantly surprised to see a number of distinctly Muslim-sounding names showing up among their team of writers. On the other hand, there's been another, more disturbing trend in recent issues: a most uncharacteristic negativity, or pessimism about the state of the world: the inevitability of food shortages, how to deal with the reality of sea level rise – and, scariest of all, a cover story entitled *'The Decline and Fall of Europe'*[10].

I'm not an economist, and I'm not privy to any inside information. Some of us thought the capitalist system was on the verge of collapse back in the 70s, but somehow it managed to keep itself going. The US Dollar, the Euro and the Pound Sterling seem remarkably strong, considering the parlous state of the economies they represent, so clearly there are issues involved beyond my ken. Nevertheless, if United Europe does survive into the third decade of the 21st century, it will, in my opinion, be more a result of good luck than good management.

The original six nations of the 1957 European Economic Community had expanded to twenty-seven by 2007. The European Commission has stated that it believes accepting countries like Bulgaria and Romania into the Union will encourage them to make the reforms needed to bring them in line with European standards – and it's becoming increasingly evident that they were wrong. There is no need for me to question the wisdom of accepting twelve new members since 2004. The current economic woes of the EU speak eloquently for themselves. I do not intend to argue for the acceptance of Turkey. I am well aware that the Commission has many reasons for postponement. However, it seems that the long-running Cyprus problem is about to blow up again, and this, I believe, is a direct result of misguided EU policies.

The Government of Turkey has announced its objections to two matters related to the Cyprus problem. The first is that the Republic of Cyprus (in fact the <u>Greek</u> republic of <u>southern</u> Cyprus) is planning to begin offshore drilling for natural gas. The second is that the aforesaid 'Republic of Cyprus' is in line to take over the rotating presidency of the EU in 2012. The Turkish Government is understandably upset, and the Minister of Foreign Affairs has conveyed their strong feelings to the EU Commissioner.

---

10 *Time Magazine*, 22 August 2011

Interestingly, the report I read referred to *'the 37-year Cyprus conflict'*, which implies that the problem began when the Turkish Government at the time sent troops to the island and established the partition which continues to this day. This line of thinking has led to international condemnation of Turkey, and recognition of part of the island as representing the whole. However, it doesn't take much research to establish that the roots of the problem go back way beyond 1974.

Like everywhere else in this part of the world, the island of Cyprus has a long history of conquests and occupation. It became a Roman province in 58 BCE, and subsequently part of the Eastern Byzantine Empire. When the Arabs began their expansion in the late 7th century, Cyprus was in the firing line, and the Byzantine emperor came to a compromise arrangement with the Muslim caliph whereby both ruled the island jointly – until the Eastern Christians were able to reassert ownership in 965 CE. As we have noted elsewhere, crusading Christians from Western Europe did not focus their aggression on Muslims alone. Ever wondered where Richard the Lionheart actually was when Robin Hood and the downtrodden English were struggling against wicked King John? It seems at least some of his time was spent conquering Cyprus (from Christians) and rescuing a French damsel-in-distress (as knights were expected to do in those days).

For the next four hundred years, Cyprus was occupied and ruled by a succession of crusaders and their hangers-on, various local potentates and Genoese mercantile interests, until finally it was purchased by the Venetians, from whom the Ottomans took it by conquest in 1571. It should be noted that, during those four centuries, the religion of the rulers was Roman Catholicism, whose adherents had little love for their Eastern Orthodox cousins, whom they persecuted and kept in subservience.

Needless to say, the Ottoman conquest was not a peaceful affair. It was pretty much standard practice in those days for conquering armies to exact revenge on the defeated populace in proportion to the amount of difficulty they had put the conquerors to. Nevertheless, the Ottomans subsequently applied their *'millet'* system to the island, whereby the Greek Orthodox community was allowed to maintain its own culture, language and religion. Without this tolerance, it is arguable that there wouldn't be a

Cyprus problem today – the island would be simply Turkish and Muslim. Take as a comparison, the situation in contemporary France and Spain, where religious dissidence was violently suppressed, resulting in homogeneous communities of (Roman Catholic) 'faith'.

So, Cyprus became Ottoman territory, and remained such for the next three centuries. Its Greek Orthodox inhabitants may not have been altogether happy, but at least they were allowed to stay, to speak their own language, practise their own religion, and within certain limits, administer their own affairs. Ottoman domination came to an end in 1878 when the British claimed the right to occupy the island. How this came about is an interesting example of 19th century European power politics. Russia is a huge country, but an ongoing historical problem has been the lack of convenient all-seasons sea access to the west. Consequently, a major focus of its expansionist drive has always been gaining access to the Black Sea, the Aegean and the Mediterranean. An important facet of Britain's foreign policy in the 19th century was preventing them from doing just that.

In 1877-78, the Ottomans were engaged in a losing war with Russia, who were altruistically supporting the nationalist struggles of Romanians and Bulgarians in the Balkans, and Armenians in eastern Anatolia. At the conclusion of this war, the European Great Powers met, at the Congress of Berlin, with the Ottoman Empire, to reorganise the Balkans, which more or less meant ejecting the Ottomans. While everyone was looking the other way, the Brits managed to insert a clause whereby they acquired 'informal' control of Cyprus. Behind this move, of course, were, the recent opening of the Suez Canal, the growing importance of oil as an energy source, and the associated inclination of Britain to consider the Mediterranean part of their own sphere of influence.

Informal control of Cyprus was formalised in 1914 when the British illegally annexed the island. The Ottomans weren't happy, but were far too occupied fighting for survival elsewhere to offer any opposition. Many Muslim Turks left the island, especially during the population exchanges at the end of the Turkish War of Independence in 1923. In the 1950s a struggle for independence began, largely involving the Greek community who wanted not only independence, but *'Enosis'* (union with mainland Greece). The British Government on its part was reluctant to surrender its strategically important military bases on the island, and opposed the insurgents, often employing local Turks as police to maintain order (thereby, needless to say, exacerbating inter-communal bitterness).

Eventually, however, the struggle was partially successful and Cyprus became an independent nation in 1960. The new constitution, guaranteed by the British, Greek and Turkish Governments, enshrined significant representative rights to the Turkish minority, somewhat reduced, but still close to twenty percent of the population. The Greeks hadn't given up, however, and the main evidence of this was their choice of Michail Christodolou Mouskos, a.k.a. Archbishop Makarios III as first president of the new republic. Hard to imagine a more provocative choice, given the saintly archbishop's well-known involvement in the Cyprus independence movement and strong support for Enosis, but there you are. Within three years he was proposing amendments to the constitution to reduce specific Turkish representation. Cypriot Turks withdrew from the government and increasing incidents of inter-communal violence broke out. Greeks from the mainland began entering Cyprus to aid the struggle for Enosis and Turks began to retreat into safer conclaves. In 1964, a United Nations peacekeeping force was set up on the island.

Over the next few years, The Turkish Government repeatedly warned the international community about violence and intimidation of the Turkish minority. There was talk but little action, and in July 1974, the military junta in mainland Greece sponsored a coup to depose the good archbishop and take over the island. Turkey's first response to this was to ask the other guarantors of Cyprus's independence, Greece and Britain, to intervene to stop renewed violence on the island. Receiving no reply, the government under Prime Minister Bülent Ecevit sent troops, and enforced partition of Cyprus into northern and southern sectors, which continue to this day. Interestingly, it was the threat of war with Turkey that led (by a process too complex to detail here) to the restoration of parliamentary democracy on the Greek mainland.

Interesting too is the fact that Great Britain (or the United Kingdom - the terminology still confuses me) retains two significant chunks of the island (in total, a little over 250 km^2) where it maintains military bases. These areas, of course, are not within the Turkish sector, though in theory they are not Greek either.

Despite all the foregoing, it is the Greek southern section of the island that is recognized by the international community, and Turkey that is continually blamed for causing and perpetuating the problem. A 1998 decision of the European Human Rights Commission held Turkey responsible for denying human rights to Greek Cypriots by preventing them from returning to their homes in Northern Cyprus. On the other hand, in 2004, the European Union admitted the (Southern, Greek) Republic of Cyprus as a member, despite a clear stipulation in the 1960 Constitution that both sectors of the Cypriot community must agree before the island could join another state. Evidently going for the letter of the law rather than its spirit, the EU decided that, since it is not actually a 'state', the condition didn't apply. Perhaps, in retrospect, Turkish Cypriots would have been better not to resign from the government back in 1963 – though, given the violence being perpetrated against their people, it's difficult to see what else they could have done.

As I mentioned earlier, it is stated policy of the EU Commission to admit countries which may not have fulfilled all the prerequisites of membership, on the principle that, once they are in, they can more easily be brought into line. Well, ask Angela Merkel if she feels that Greece and Ireland, Spain and Portugal made much effort to bring their economies into line with EU requirements after joining. As for the 'Republic of Cyprus', it's hard to escape the feeling that international and EU acceptance has merely hardened their attitude to their Turkish brethren in the north. United Nations Secretaries-General, Boutros Boutros Ghali and Kofi Annan, both proposed peace settlements for the Cyprus issue. The most recent of these, the Annan Plan (2002), was accepted by the Turkish Government and the people of Turkish northern Cyprus in a referendum, but rejected by the Greeks in the south.

Once again the Cyprus issue is making headlines around the world. The Turkish Government is vociferously objecting to Greek Cypriot plans to conduct natural gas exploration in waters off the coast, and to the likelihood that Greek Cyprus will provide the next EU President. It is unlikely that Turkey would be prepared to go to war over either of these issues, given that they would undoubtedly be warned off by Europe and the USA. However, it is a sign of Turkey's increasing confidence in the region that its government is prepared to take the initiative on the Cyprus issue rather than continuing to accept a defensive pariah role. If the international community decides to take a more even-handed approach to solving the problem, Mr Erdoğan and his government will probably consider the risk to have been worthwhile.

5

Atatürk's Republic and the Wall Street Protesters

16 October 2011

One of the peculiarities that most strikes visitors to Turkey is the pervasive presence of a political leader who died more than seventy years ago. Every classroom in every school, every office in every government department has his picture on the wall; every public square in every village, town and city has a statue prominently placed. Our tendency is to feel that there must be an element of compulsion involved. How can a free people willingly engage in such idolatry? Certainly other nations have their founding heroes, but I can think of none who holds the place in his people's hearts that Mustafa Kemal Atatürk holds in the hearts of the people of Turkey.

Perhaps the nearest rival is George Washington, whose pictorial place on the US dollar bill symbolises his importance as founding father of the United States. The English have two queens with particular claims to fame: Elizabeth I, the mother of England, and Victoria, of the British Empire – but nobody much hangs their pictures on the wall these days. Cross the Channel to Europe and you've got Napoleon Bonaparte in

France. However, since he set back republican progress for the best part of a century, you might question his achievement. Prior to him, you have to go back to the 9th century to find a French leader of much note, but who's heard of Charlemagne these days, much less knows what he did? Germany has a more recent claimant (if we tactfully ignore Adolf Hitler). Otto von Bismarck was the driving force uniting the German nation in 1871, and you'd have to say Europe would be in much deeper trouble these days without the Germans. Peter the Great did a lot of big stuff for Russia back around 1700, but I don't know what the Russians think of him now. Outside of Europe? Well, Gandhi in India, of course, and Nelson Mandela in South Africa; hard to find fault with them. The Chinese might suggest Mao Zedong, and Fidel Castro was the public face of Cuba for most of fifty years. That's quite a club to join, isn't it!

But how do you rank them? What criteria would you use to determine their impact on the world? If you go for population size of their countries, Gandhi and Mao Zedong top the list. On the other hand, if you think in terms of global economic and military power today, and the lasting effects of his legacy, it's hard to go past George Washington. When it comes to personal sacrifice and commitment to a cause, Mandela, and once again, Gandhi look pretty good. Take the business model of time and motion effectiveness and Bismarck got the job done quickly, which suggests impressive personal power and influence.

Now I'm sure many outside Turkey will ask how a Turkish leader, however idolized in his own country, can be considered fit to stand in such company. Well, leaving the idolization aside for a moment, you may not be aware that the United Nations and UNESCO declared 1981 (the centennial year of his birth) as *Atatürk Year in the World*, the only occasion on which they have awarded such an honour. The wording of the 1979 resolution goes like this[11]:

---

11 http://en.wikipedia.org/wiki/Atatürk_Centennial

The General Conference,
Convinced that eminent personalities who worked for international under-
standing, co-operation, and peace, should serve as an example for future
generations,
Recalling that the hundredth anniversary of the birth of Mustafa Kemal
Atatürk, the founder of the Republic of Turkey, will be celebrated in 1981,
Bearing in mind that he was an exceptional reformer in all the fields coming
within UNESCO's competence,
Recognizing in particular that he was the leader of one of the earliest struggles
against colonialism and imperialism,
Recalling that he set an outstanding example in promoting the spirit of mutual
understanding between peoples and lasting peace between the nations of the
world, having advocated all his life the advent of 'an age of harmony and co-
operation in which no distinction would be made between men on account of
colour, religion or race',

1. Decides that UNESCO shall co-operate on the intellectual and technical
planes with the Turkish Government for the organization in 1980, at that
Government's financial expense, of an international symposium designed to
bring out various aspects of the personality and work of Atatürk, the founder of
the Republic of Turkey, whose action was always directed towards the promotion
of peace, international understanding and respect for human rights;

2. Requests the Director-General to take the necessary steps for the
implementation of this resolution.

Well, that would seem to take care of the question of international recognition. Nelson Mandela has been named a UN Goodwill Ambassador,
and UNESCO issued a commemorative medal to mark the 125th anniversary of Mahatma Gandhi's birth – but neither, as far as I know, has yet
been accorded a 'Year' to himself. So let's return to the reasons why Atatürk
remains so beloved by the Turkish people, and I want to draw your particular attention to these words from the UN resolution: *'he was an excep-*
tional reformer in all the fields coming within UNESCO's competence'. These

fields are summarized by the letters ESC in the acronym: *'Educational, Scientific and Cultural'*. So clearly the people at the UN had other factors in mind than mere military success when they decided to honour Atatürk. Books have been written on this subject, so for the purposes of this article, I want to focus on one aspect – his achievements in the field of economics.

Undoubtedly, Mustafa Kemal's military successes, achieved against global military powers of the day, were remarkable. Nevertheless, he himself recognized the limitations of victory gained by force of arms. The report of the Turkish Ministry of Finance for 2011 leads off with these words attributed to Atatürk:

'The greatest political and military victory cannot last and is doomed to fade away quickly unless it is crowned by an economic victory.'

It is appropriate, then, to glance briefly at the Turkey which gained its status as an independent republic in 1923. The first thing to recognise is that the new Turkey was the rump of the old Ottoman Empire, a once proud entity that had become the plaything of European powers, and a laughing-stock for its social, cultural, technological and economic backwardness. The Anatolian heartland comprised around twenty percent of the territory of the Ottoman Empire in 1914, and a minute fraction of its greatest extent in the 17th century. When it became the Republic of Turkey in 1923 it had been devastated by ten consecutive years of war on fronts on all its boundaries. The total population was around thirteen million and productive manpower was severely depleted. Adult literacy was less than twenty percent and there were nearly 13,000 people for every doctor. The Republic had been achieved, but the economy was in tatters. Building a modern developed nation required a vision and a mechanism.

Mustafa Kemal's economic mechanism was 'statism' (Turkish *devletçilik*). The essence of this is that *the state has a major and legitimate role in directing the economy, either directly through state-owned enterprises and other types of machinery of government, or indirectly through economic planning*[12]. His vision was an educated population with an improved standard of living for all, and a nation free from foreign control. It was, we may say, the *'Third Way'*, so sought after (but sadly, not found) by New Labour politicians and pseudo-leftists of the Tony Blair variety – avoiding the pitfalls of Socialism/ Communism on the one hand, and unfettered free market capitalism on the other. To the extent that Turkey under Atatürk vastly improved internal communications (including new and improved roads and railways), quadrupled electricity generation, and greatly increased agricultural and industrial production, we can say his policies were successful.

An interesting question, of course, is how he managed to achieve these successes. Money does not grow on trees, as we are often told – and within six years of the foundation of the Turkish Republic, the world was plunged into a catastrophic economic Depression. Now I'm not going to pretend that I know where the money came from, but I want to share with you some things I do know about that period of world history, in which Atatürk was an important and well-informed participant.

I have just been reading *'A History of Economics'* by the eminent American economist, John Kenneth Galbraith. It's getting little old now, since it was published back in 1987, but I think, as an observer of our world in economic terms, Galbraith pretty much hits the spot – and his predictions for the future have a ring of truth when tested against our own experience of the last decades. He explains why classical orthodox economic thought was so helpless in the face of the Great Depression. Simply put, the Depression shouldn't have happened. In an ideal free market world, prices, wages, investment, interest, and production all balance each other out at their optimum level. Leave it to the market, and all will be fine. But it wasn't, of course, as five or six years of the laissez-faire approach served to show. In the end, it was the English economist, John Maynard Keynes,

---

12 *Wikipedia* quoting the *Routledge Encyclopedia of International Political Economy*

coupled with the economic stimulus of the Second World War that got the world into the good years of the 50s and 60s. Keynes it was who sanctified deficit spending, whereby governments were permitted, nay, encouraged, to push-start their moribund economies by spending beyond their income, the gap to be bridged by private-sector borrowing. Keynes's legacy lives on, despite the ranting of conservatives for balanced budgets. The USA is far and away the largest debtor-nation on Earth.

Something you won't find in such histories of economics is reference to a debate that shook the world of finance in the 1920s and 30s, and continued in some countries well into the 50s and 60s. This was the question of where money actually comes from. As Galbraith says, and everyone knows who pauses to think for a moment, 'money' is not an easy concept to tie down. Clearly the notes and coins in our wallets are a small part of it. There are the bank deposits that we may or may not choose to call on with our chequebooks and ATM cards. There are the credit cards with their generous limits that we may or may not choose to make use of. There are the personal loans for cars, houses and holidays that my bank often offers me, of which I may or may not avail myself. Some economic thinkers and politicians after the First World War were of the opinion that what they called the 'nation's credit' should be under the sole control of the state.

I want to inject a little New Zealand history here, since that is what I am most familiar with. At the height of the Great Depression, in 1935, New Zealanders, in desperation, elected their first ever Labour Government. The leader of that government, Prime Minister Michael Joseph Savage, is undoubtedly the nearest thing we have to an 'Atatürk' in our history. Twenty and even thirty years later, pictures of that saintly man were still to be found hanging in the houses of grateful citizens. A large mausoleum stands to his memory in a park in one of Auckland's most beautiful locations. Savage's fame rests primarily on one achievement: the building of a large store of state houses. The project employed thousands of New Zealanders at a time when unemployment was at a disastrous level; stimulated industrial production at a time when there was no money for investment; and provided low-rental, good quality accommodation for previously impoverished and ill-housed citizens. In the eyes of ordinary New Zealanders, Savage was a worthy candidate for beatification!

The thing is, it wasn't really Savage who did it. The mostly forgotten architect of the scheme was a First World War hero, charismatic orator and self-educated economics whiz kid by the name of John A Lee. Despite being a major factor in the Labour Government's electoral success, he was over-looked for ministerial appointment, and thrown the under-secretaryship of housing as a consolation. Seizing his chance, Lee persuaded his cabinet colleagues to authorize the provision of Reserve Bank credit (ie new money) at minimal interest to finance the housing project. It was the one and only time such a measure was used. NZ's Finance minister was summoned to London, where it is thought he was told by political and financial leaders to toe the orthodox line in future. Lee, who refused to cooperate, was expelled from the Labour Party – and subsequent Labour Governments have fallen into the accepted borrow-and-hope mould.

But it wasn't just an isolated incident. Canadians especially liked the Social Credit (as it became known) financial concept, and public pressure forced the government to set up a Royal Commission on Banking and Currency in 1933. Continuing electoral support for the idea obliged the New Zealand Government to follow a similar course in 1955. Both Royal Commissions acknowledged that money creation is, in fact, a function of the private banking system, rather than the sovereign right of the state, as most people naively continue to believe. It has been suggested that Keynesian deficit financing was a direct response to, and an at-tempt to destroy the momentum of the monetary reformists. If so, it was largely successful. *'Money is power'*[13], and these days, the idea has pretty much disappeared from sight or public interest. Present-day US citizens attempting to invade Wall Street, and like-minded souls protesting in cities throughout the world against the immorality and social destruc-tiveness of the activities of the financial sector know what they are angry

---

13 A quote attributed to Russell H. Conwell, Baptist minister and founder of Temple University, Philadelphia

about – but unfortunately have no rallying philosophy or mechanism to offer as an alternative.

That's another reason why we need to take another look at Mustafa Kemal Atatürk and his generation of thinkers from the 1920s and 30s. Atatürk must have had almost unlimited opportunity to amass a personal fortune and establish a political or financial dynasty – but he didn't do it. He divorced his only wife, sired no children (as far as we know), and his surname died with him. I would like to leave you with three quotations from the store of wisdom the man left to us:

- *Social status is of no use to the nation – service is the thing. Whoever serves the nation has the highest status.*

- *Educators, what our republic needs from you is young people who can think, know right from wrong, and have open minds.*

- *War can only be just or justified if it is fought out of sheer necessity or for reasons of national defence, or pursued by a people awaiting their sovereignty, their very lives depending on it.*

6

Vikings in Constantinople - Globalisation then and now

13 November 2011

Globalisation is an interesting business, with positive and negative effects on all aspects of life in our contemporary world. Most of us tend to think of it as a modern phenomenon, when, in fact, the process has been going on since time immemorial. Polynesian migrants, originating in Asia, traversed thousands of kilometres of trackless Pacific Ocean, eventually finding their way to New Zealand, perhaps the last significant land mass in the world to be populated.

The territory currently occupied by modern Turkey, on the other hand, has long been at the focal point of mass migrations of humanity. Not everyone is aware, however, that Vikings, those widely wandering wayfarers, found their way down the navigable rivers of Eastern Europe to the Black Sea and the largest city of the medieval world, establishing a presence there a thousand years before their modern descendants from Northern Europe flocked to the beach resorts of Mediterranean Turkey. I've always had a penchant for historical fiction. As a kid, one of my favourite writers was Henry Treece, whose 'Viking' Trilogy included a novel entitled *'The Road to Miklagard'*. Check it out! Not only did those hairy guys with the horned helmets discover America centuries before Christopher Columbus, they also had several goes at conquering Constantinople from the Byzantine Greeks, and if you can believe some sources, actually founded Russia in their spare time.

Like Turks, Vikings have tended to get a bad press over the years. Raping and pillaging seem to have been standard male activities for most of recorded history, so it is perhaps a little unfair to single out Vikings (and Turks) for special mention. On the plus side of the ledger, the Vikings had a pretty significant influence on much of Europe from the 8th to the 11th century, to the extent that that period of European history is often referred to as *'The Viking Age'*. Certainly they propelled those distinctive dragon-prowed long-ships to some quite surprising places. Advanced ship-building techniques such as the development of the keel, and clinker-built construction, in conjunction with sophisticated systems of navigation, enabled them to travel regularly to Iceland, Greenland and the east coast of North America.

For sure, the Viking reputation for violent invasion of other people's territory is not undeserved. They actually managed to lay siege to Paris for a whole year in the late 9th century – eventually having to be bought off by a couple of French Kings, remembered by historians as Charles the Fat and Charles the Simple. You can't help wondering who would have given kings such unflattering epithets – their own disgruntled subjects? Or perhaps a gang of triumphant Vikings at a drunken after-battle celebration. Anyway, as a result, a significant chunk of northwestern France became known as Normandy (land of the Northmen) whose inhabitants famously conquered the English in 1066, and may be said to have exerted a civilising influence on the local Anglo-Saxons. Certainly their monumental Romanesque architecture, and their idiosyncratic dialect of French left lasting impressions on English cathedrals and the language of English law.

Well, Leif Ericson's achievement in crossing the Atlantic and setting foot in North America is no longer controversial. Some modern Americans apparently go so far as to commemorate his feat on 9 October each year.

Modern Russians, however, are understandably reluctant to accept that the origin of their very name is Scandinavian; still less that they owe the foundation of their nation to the Vikings. Nevertheless, there exists a persuasive argument . . .

The name *'Rus'* referred originally to Swedish Vikings who, in the 8th and 9th centuries, found their way to Eastern Europe and what is now northern Russia. Needless to say, their practice of exacting tribute did not always endear them to the locals. Nevertheless, it seems that indigenous Slavic and Finnish tribes, unable to agree amongst themselves, actually invited a certain Viking lord by the name of Rurik, to come and rule them – this around the end of the 9th century. The result, according to some historians, was the establishment of a proto-state, Kievan Rus, which eventually evolved into modern Russia. Slavic historians, on the contrary, are not keen on this theory; and they have, on their side, an absence of signs of lasting linguistic or cultural influence remaining from the Scandinavian presence.

I have no intention of entering into the controversy, for the reasons that I'm not a historian and I don't particularly care either way. However, it does seem to me that, from what we know of Vikings, they were not especially interested in, or temperamentally suited to, putting down roots and investing the kind of long-term energy required to enforce their language and culture on local peoples. Some small linguistic peculiarities do survive in modern English, from the time when Viking invaders made their presence felt on England's eastern coast – but on the whole it seems that the Viking way was to move on to greener and more immediately profitable pastures. Those who remained behind tended to be assimilated into the local culture. We have already noted the Norman adoption of the French language – and it seems the Vikings who settled in what is now Russia, also adopted Slavic customs and language.

But getting back to Henry Treece, and the point of this post – the Vikings apparently referred collectively to the towns and forts they established in what is now northern Russia as *Gardariki*. From there, the more adventurous among them found their way down the Volga and Dnieper River systems to the Caspian and Black Seas, where they inevitably came into contact with the top dogs in that part of the world, the Byzantine Graeco-Romans. Undeterred by the size and reputation of the Byzantine Empire, the upstart Scandinavians apparently launched several attacks on the great city of Constantinople (which they called *Miklagard*) in the 9th and 10th centuries.

These attacks were unsuccessful, of course, but they did have the result of obliging the Byzantines to develop a healthy respect for these blond berserkers from the frozen north. It was around this time that the rising power of the Muslim Arabs to the south was beginning to pose a more serious threat to the Empire. With admirable pragmatism, the Emperor Theophilus began the tradition of employing Viking hatchet men in defence of his realm. Thus was founded the so-called Varangian Guard, which, in later years became the personal bodyguard of the Emperor Basil II and his successors. Evidently there was considerable too-ing and fro-ing between Scandinavia and Asia Minor, with Viking mercenaries sending at least some of their earnings home, before heading back to retire in comfort. It is said that this occupation was so enticing to young warriors that the King of Sweden felt obliged to pass a law preventing his subjects from inheriting property while working for the 'Greek' Emperors.

Once again, not much evidence has survived of the presence of these Norsemen in the Near East. There is, however, an interesting item of graffiti in the cathedral church of Hagia Sophia, now the Aya Sofia Museum in Istanbul. Carved into the marble balustrade of one of the galleries is a runic inscription (dated to some time in the 11th century) recording the presence of a certain Halfdan – who, one assumes, was finding the ceremonial rites of the Orthodox Church a little tiresome. At the other end of the journey, two rune stones, also dating from the 11th century, have been found at Risbyle in Sweden. The stones bear inscriptions to the memory of Ulfr of Skolhamarr, and one of them, it seems, includes an Eastern Cross, common in the Byzantine Empire at the time. To commemorate the international connection, the local Swedish municipality has apparently included such a cross in its official coat-of-arms.

As a final twist to this story, it seems that the Varangian Guard began to lose its Viking character in the 11th century. Around this time, the ranks of the Imperial bodyguard began increasingly to be filled by Anglo-Saxon warriors from England. Interestingly, however, the Vikings were also, albeit obliquely, responsible for this trend. Apparently the depredations of Vikings in England, and later, the conquest of the country by their kinsmen the Normans, led to considerable dispossession, redundancy and unemployment of the native English warrior class – many of whom, it is said, took their services elsewhere, namely, to the court of the Byzantine Emperor in Constantinople.

Now, if you have read this far, you will be aware that one of my major themes is the inter-connectedness of historical events. I have written elsewhere about the Crusades, and my feeling that Papal motives went beyond the normally stated objective of reclaiming the Holy Lands from the heathen Turks. As I was writing the above, it crossed my mind that there, in the 11th century, you had significant numbers of middle and upper-middle class guys from England and other parts of western Europe getting a glimpse of the wealth of Eastern civilisation, and re-turning to tell tales of its splendour to the folks back home. So, when Pope Urban II made his famous call, in 1095, to Western Christendom to unite in arms and make the three thousand kilometre journey to lib-erate the Holy Places, there may well have been thoughts of material as much as spiritual gain in the minds of those noble knights and true. Such thoughts could conceivably have added persuasive force to the Holy Father's arguments.

Well, the more things change, the more they remain the same, as the French say. The US government is currently working towards a withdrawal of its troops from Iraq, as Britain also seeks to cut back its military presence abroad. You might wonder, then, why so many Americans and other for-eign nationals would opt voluntarily to go to Iraq and engage in the kind of activities that normally only trained soldiers would carry out. The rea-sons, of course, are money and adventure. In August 2010 it was estimated that there were in excess of eleven thousand *private security contractors* (read 'mercenaries') in Iraq – and analysts expect that number to rise significantly as US military withdrawal continues.

So, the Vikings went to Miklagard, the Crusaders to Jerusalem (and Constantinople), and Americans will, no doubt, continue going to Iraq. The processes of globalisation, and its handmaiden, privatisation, are timeless and irresistible. But let's not kid ourselves that they spring from altruism and benevolence towards anyone's fellow human beings.

7

Dersim and the Politics of Inclusion

10 December 2011

I first came to Turkey just after Mel Gibson and his team won five Oscars for their 1995 cinematic hit, *'Braveheart'*. For some reason that romanticised tale of kilted Scots fighting manfully but futilely against their powerful southern neighbour struck a chord or two with Turkish audiences. The film ran for three years in Istanbul cinemas without a break. *'Titanic'* didn't come close in this part of the world!

I'm sure you remember the final stomach-churning scenes of the film, where the defeated but unrepentant William Wallace is hanged, drawn and quartered by his English conquerors as an example to others who might seek to emulate his troublesome ways. Wallace's tormentor gives him the option of a quick death on condition of swearing allegiance to His Majesty, the King of England. However, the Scots hero draws strength to undergo the agony ahead from a small boy in the crowd, who will clearly carry on the fight if Gibson (sorry, Wallace) shows the necessary fortitude.

Scotland was an independent nation in those days – we're talking about the early 14th century – so it was perhaps a bit rough to treat Wallace as a traitor. Nevertheless, that gruesome punishment remained in force in the

United Kingdom for the crime of high treason into comparatively modern times. The Crowns and Parliaments of Scotland had been well united by the time Prince Charlie led his ill-fated rebellion against King George II in 1745. It was only sixty years since his grandfather, James II, had allowed Judge Jeffreys to butcher survivors of the Monmouth Rebellion, so the Bonny Prince knew what to expect if he was caught. He wasn't, luckily for him (speeding off to the Isle of Skye on his bonny boat, as the old song has it, and thence to a life of exile in France), but the Scots Highlanders who had supported him were not so fortunate. The Battle of Culloden lasted just over an hour, say the records. However, the aftermath of the English victory was not only a massacre of the wounded, but a prolonged killing or displacement of the clansmen, their women, children and the elderly. It was a systematic programme, more or less successful, to civilise the highlands, bring them under the rule of law, and to suppress the Gaelic language and tribal culture.

Hanging drawing and quartering was apparently not considered a seemly punishment for women, for whom burning was the favoured punishment in those times. The last burning in England took place in 1789 – the year of the French Revolution (*'Liberty, Equality and Brotherhood'*, you remember!). The more anatomically specific alternative for males remained in force rather longer. The last man in England to suffer the fate of William Wallace was hanged and beheaded in 1817. Several more fortunate rebels actually faced the penalty in 1839 – but their sentence was commuted to transportation, and butchering as a punishment was finally removed from British law in 1870.

Well, that's all very interesting, I hear you say, but what relevance does it have for the post-modern world. Even Turkey, with its reputation for human rights abuses, could not possibly condone such treatment of political prisoners or even terrorists. And you'd be right. Capital punishment itself was abolished completely in Turkey in 2004.

Nevertheless, an event in 20th century Turkish history has recently seen the light of day, and warrants a little examination. Dersim, now known as Tunceli, is an area in eastern central Anatolia, traditionally home to Alevi, Zaza and Kurdish people. According to one source I came across, this was the last area within the Turkish Republic to be brought under government control. It is not easy to come to a clear understanding of who these people are. Kurds are an ancient race, of Iranian origin, speaking a language with Indo-European roots. Many of them espouse the Alevi branch of Islam, held to spring from the *Shi'a* sect (not of much consequence in *Sunni* majority Turkey), but with connections to earlier religions and much older folk traditions. Zazas, it seems, generally incline to Alevism, but there is scholarly debate about whether their language is related to Kurdish, or distinct from it.

Be that as it may, it seems that the inhabitants of Dersim/Tunceli had been resisting all attempts to bring them into the fold of civilisation for some time before the watershed events of 1937-38. According to van Bruinessen[14],

'the only law they recognized was traditional tribal law. Tribal chieftains and religious leaders wielded great authority over the commoners, whom they often exploited economically. They were not opposed to government as such, as long as it did not interfere too much in their affairs . . . There was a tradition of refusing to pay taxes — but then there was little that could be taxed, as the district was desperately poor. Young men evaded military service when they could . . .'

Undoubtedly there was a certain amount of brigandage and banditry, and government attempts to impose the rule of law may have met with actual physical discouragement. We may think that the situation was similar to that of the Scottish Highland clans prior to the final solution discussed above, with one major difference: we are talking about the 20th century here, rather than the 18th. The Turkish Republic was a mere fourteen years old, and in a pretty parlous state. Republican reformers, led by Mustafa Kemal Atatürk, were attempting to forge a nation from the ashes of the defeated, divided and defunct Ottoman Empire. They were trying to create an identity based on the hitherto unpopular concept of Turkish nationalism; to establish a modern, secular democracy in a land whose

---

14 *'The Suppression of the Dersim Rebellion in Turkey (1937-38)'*, Martin van Bruinessen

tradition was Islamic, monarchic and borderline medieval. Their eyes were fixed on European models of civilisation, most of whose representatives had long since suppressed and/or civilized their last remnants of nomadic or pastoral tribalism.

Furthermore, we are talking about the 1930s, not a period much re-nowned for the tolerant treatment of troublesome and undesirable minori-ties. So what happened in Dersim? It seems the government of the day made attempts to assimilate the Alevi Zazas into their brave new secular civilized Turkish Republic - and the local tribes objected, to the point of open rebellion. The government, needless to say, had recourse to military coercion. Many died, villages were destroyed, local people were displaced, martial law was established, there was a general ban on the Kurdish lan-guage, dress, folklore and names, and, as one would expect, a good deal of anger and enmity continued to seethe underground. Well, you can't make a civilisation omelette without breaking a few eggs, it seems.

So what's the solution? The present day government of New Zealand is not about to hand *Aotearoa* back to its indigenous Maori inhabitants; just as the British government continues to resist attempts by Scottish national-ists to cede from the Union and go it alone. No Turkish government will ever accept the handing over of its eastern provinces to an independent Kurdistan, even if the majority of 'Kurds' wanted it – something which is by no means certain. However, the Turkish Prime Minister, Mr Erdoğan, recently apologized publically for the events known collectively as the *'Dersim Massacre'*.

It's a step in the right direction, isn't it! You can't ever right the wrongs of history. History itself is a progression of successive societies, chieftains, monarchs, invaders and whatnot, asserting their pre-eminence, and impos-ing their will on others by the right of might – irrespective of whether the 'others' may have had a prior and better claim to the territory in question. Nevertheless, smart leaders of the victorious party tend to apply the prin-ciple of enlightened self-interest. The new nation you seek to establish, the new civilisation whose superiority you assert, will have a better chance of long-term success if you give the conquered people a share of its fruits.

Nelson Mandela understood this when he became the first democratically elected President of the Republic of South Africa in 1994. Mandela had spent twenty-seven years of his life in prison, a victim of the *apartheid* political system that allowed white people, making up ten percent of the population, to rule and oppress the non-white ninety percent It would have been understandable if he had taken the opportunity to exact revenge from his persecutors, now that he was in power – but he didn't. He encouraged his people to work on a process of reconciliation, to heal the wounds of the past and take the reborn nation forward.

The Ottoman Empire, for all its failings, survived for more than six centuries, and one reason for its longevity may have been the *millet* system, whereby it granted freedom of religion, use of language and practising of traditions to the disparate groups within its borders: Orthodox Greeks, Armenians and Jews, as well as Muslims of all shades. The British Empire may have been geographically the largest the world has known, but even the most generous historian would not grant it a span of much more than three hundred years. More realistically, the 19th century and twenty or thirty years either side of it would encompass its actual period of dominant power. Interestingly, the British one was probably the only Empire that never had an Emperor. Its subjects owed fealty to the King (or Queen) of England – a rather remote concept for most of them, and the requirement to accept a homogeneity of language and culture may have hastened the empire's demise.

But I'm not here to criticize the Brits. My purpose is to congratulate Mr Tayyip Erdoğan for his efforts in reaching out to the unhappy Kurds and Zazas among the citizens of Turkey. Admittedly, his motives have been called into question by some. He has been accused of taking advantage of a sensitive issue to score points against his main political rival, Kemal Kılıçdaroğlu, whose family apparently has Kurdish/Alevi origins in the Tunceli/Dersim area. Well, it's an unusual politician who does not avail himself of an opportunity to make political capital, and I'm not going into that matter either. Mr Erdoğan's words will be measured against his actions in the future. Any apology for past wrongs will be hollow without governmental measures to extend financial support to Turkey's impoverished and disadvantaged citizens in the east, many of whom are Kurdish. Schools and hospitals are needed, and industrial development to provide employment opportunities. Poverty and deprivation are the soil in which rebellion and terrorism flourish. Alleviating these conditions will not make all the malcontents disappear overnight – but it will at least deprive them of a receptive audience.

In February 2008, the former Prime Minister of Australia, Mr Kevin Rudd, made a formal apology to the aboriginal people for more than a century of cruelty, oppression and marginalization inflicted on them by successive governments. It's too early to say whether Mr Rudd's words will result in action to reduce the dreadful rates of infant mortality, educational failure and unemployment, alcoholism and drug abuse, petty crime and imprisonment, among Australia's indigenous people – but certainly, without recognition and apology, nothing can change.

I want to make two points here. The first is that, unfortunately, no civilized society can tolerate outlaws, despite their traditional romantic appeal. Pretty much every modern civilized society you care to examine has, somewhere in its history, an event or two where it felt obliged to use force to suppress a group whose continued existence was perceived as a serious threat to its own integrity and stability. We've mentioned the United Kingdom and Turkey, Australia and New Zealand. We could go on to look at the United States' treatment of Native Americans, or its catastrophic Civil War, fought to prevent a division into Union and Confederacy – but you get the gist. My second point is that such use of force can, however, only be justified in the long-term if the result is a stable civilized inclusive state, the benefits of which extend to the majority of its citizens.

The Republic of Turkey has, since its inception, looked to the West as a model of cultural and economic development, of democracy and civilisation. The West, for its part, has often chosen to judge and belittle Turkey for its perceived backwardness and barbarity. It is important, then, for Western nations, if they are to maintain the moral high ground, that their civilized democratic institutions demonstrate a capacity for inclusion. Unfortunately, recent events seem to suggest that they do not. 'Occupy Wall

St' protests have spread to major cities all over the developed world, suggesting a 'Capitalist Spring' (or 'Autumn') that has elicited outbursts of government force to suppress it. One of the rallying cries has been 'We are the 99%' – the supposed proportion of society held in economic servitude to the 1% elite.

I don't have the numbers at my fingertips, but I have to say that I feel a 99:1 split may be exaggerating the situation a little. However, one statistic I did come across in the last week gave cause for alarm. A General Election was held in New Zealand the weekend before last, and reports are saying that voter turnout was, at sixty-five percent, the lowest in more than a century. Certainly, the implication that thirty-five percent of the voting-age population are so disaffected that they do not bother to exercise their democratic right is disturbing. General Elections in the UK in recent years have produced a similar ominous trend. Figures in the USA are even more striking. Statistics show[15] that the proportion of eligible voters turning out to choose a new President hovers around fifty to fifty-five percent. If you look at mid-term Congressional elections the percentage drops below forty!

Well, it would require more exhaustive research than I have time for, to demonstrate a clear correlation between these voting patterns and the August riots in UK cities, the Wall St protesters, the general increase in terrorist activity around the globe, and the huge popularity of movies with anti-establishment heroes like William Wallace. All I can say for certain is that I applaud Tayyip Erdoğan for extending a hand of apology and reconciliation to the victims of the Dersim rebellion - and I fervently hope that his words translate into actions which will achieve a more equitable distribution of wealth in his rapidly developing nation.

---

15 http://www.infoplease.com/ipa/A0781453.html

8

Tales of Smugglers and Indirect Taxation - The Şırnak Incident

3 January 2012

No doubt you saw news coverage of the deaths of thirty-five villagers in southeastern Turkey. According to reports, a convoy of young Kurdish smugglers was making its way by night towards the Turkish border leading donkeys laden with contraband petrol and cigarettes from neighbouring Iraq. Their presence was detected by military drones and thermal cameras, and they were taken for Kurdish insurgents belonging to the outlawed PKK, who apparently often use that border crossing to launch strikes against Turkish police and military targets from their bases in the mountains of Iraq. In a tragic case of being in the wrong place at the wrong time, the smugglers were strafed and bombed by Turkish warplanes. Reports say most of the dead were young men around seventeen to twenty years old.

The incident is a major embarrassment for the Turkish government, who have been pursuing a dual policy of hitting 'terrorists' hard, while trying to defuse the separatist issue by allowing discussion on the use of the Kurdish language and the practising of the Alevi religion. Political opponents, needless to say, have seen a golden opportunity to attack the

government, making comparisons to the killing of dissidents by beleaguered President Bashar al-Assad in neighbouring Syria.

I made a journey into that southeastern part of Turkey back in the
summer of 1999. In retrospect, I was fortunate because, at that time, there
was a brief window of relative peace following the arrest and imprisonment of PKK leader, Abdullah Öcalan, and before George 'Dubya' Bush's
invasion of Iraq stirred up Kurdish activists again. I didn't get right down
to that distant corner of Anatolia, to Hakkari and Şırnak, where the latest
incident took place, but I did make my way deep into parts of the country
with Kurdish majority populations: Malatya, Diyarbakır, Mardin and Van.
Despite the relative calm, we faced regular stoppages at checkpoints, with
tanks and other serious-looking military hardware very much in evidence.

There were very few tourists – I met a group of young back-packers
from Poland in Doğubeyazit, way out on the border with Iran, but saw no
others. I was able to make a small contribution to international goodwill
in that remote town, purchasing a New Zealand twenty-dollar bill from a
taxi driver who would have waited a long time for another such opportunity. Since hostilities resumed after 2003, I imagine the tourist trade has, if
anything, declined. Certainly the New Zealand Embassy in Ankara sends
out emails to ex-pat citizens and tourists warning us to avoid those parts
of the country.

These hostilities are another instance of what we have come to know
as asymmetrical warfare – where a professional national military machine
combats groups of irregular guerrillas. We have read much about the post-
traumatic stress disorder afflicting US servicemen returning from tours of
duty in Iraq. One major cause of this stress, no doubt, is that, in such asymmetrical conflicts, the professional soldiers suffer from the disadvantage of
having to wear a uniform, making them clearly identifiable targets. On the
other hand, local guerrillas are not easily distinguished from harmless civilians, especially when you don't speak the local language. As a result, the pro-
fessionals are in a state of constant fear and uncertainty, and not infrequently
kill or wound non-combatant citizens going about their lawful business.

Well, I'm not excusing the Turkish military for what they did down
there in Uludere, in Şırnak province. However, the situation is, you'd have

to say, somewhat complex. For a start, the victims of the air-strike were Turkish citizens intending to re-cross an international border, having, we must assume, previously left the country without notifying the proper authorities, for a purpose which could hardly be called lawful business, and this in the dead of night. Moreover, the path they were on is apparently used by PKK insurgents making guerrilla raids into Turkey from bases across the border in Iraq. Certainly those guys were too young to die, and the price they paid was disproportionate to their crime – but they were surely old enough to know the risk they were taking.

However, that's not much consolation for those families in Uludere who have lost the flower of their local manhood – and it is certainly creating extra unpleasantness for the Turkish government in relations with their Kurdish citizens, even if they do fulfil their promise to pay substantial reparations. Still, ascribing blame is always a difficult task, and knee-jerk responses rarely address the underlying causes of a conflict, so let's take a step back . . .

The Turkish Republic has one of the world's booming economies these days. The middle class is expanding rapidly, the retail sector is on a roll, private sector commercial and residential construction is changing the urban skyline, and the government is proceeding with numerous large-scale public projects. They do, however, have some difficulties in collecting taxation. No one likes paying tax, of course, but not paying it is a way of life in Turkey. Collecting income tax from wage and salary earners is relatively straightforward – but what if the company doesn't declare its employees? And getting tax out of the wealthy is notoriously problematic, even in countries with more reliable bureaucratic infrastructure.

One widely employed solution is indirect taxation. Everybody does it these days: GST, VAT, KDV . . . a nettle by any other name would sting as sharp. And then there are the special purpose taxes. Who can argue with extra duties on cigarettes and alcohol? If people want to drink and smoke themselves to death, why should I pay for their health care with my taxes? And petrol . . . well, drivers should contribute to the cost of roads and motorways and whatnot, it's only fair and reasonable.

Turkey, however, is a special case. I read that Americans got upset when the price of gasoline reached $4 a gallon. Imagine the screams of outrage if they had to pay $8.50, as Turkish motorists do! They'd never get the protesters out of the parks! And if the US Federal Government tried to take seventy percent of the price in tax, the Tea Party would likely be organising airstrikes on the White House.

Then there's the cigarette tax. There was a time when 'to smoke like a Turk' was axiomatic. Now I'm starting to feel sorry for Turkish smokers, who currently pay nine Turkish liras or more for a packet of smokes, of which 7.50 TL goes to the government. Unlike smoking, however, drinking is not such a big thing in Turkey. In tea consumption, Turks are right up there with the English – but Islam has traditionally frowned on alcohol. The land that probably invented wine production allowed the art to die out until the last decade or so saw some kind of revival.

The exception to this abstemiousness has been rakı, the grape-based, aniseed-flavoured spirit resembling Greek ouzo, which is a popular accompaniment to a Turkish night on the town. Perhaps I should have said 'was', since a litre bottle of the cheapest *Yeni Rakı* now retails for 61 TL, of which sixty-two percent disappears into government coffers.

So what's the connection, you're saying. The Turkish military kills thirty-five poor young villagers out east, and I'm blethering on about the price of grog and cigarettes. But don't be hasty. It's pretty clear that those kids were smuggling cigarettes and petrol. Of course it's illegal, but when people take such risks to do it, you can safely bet that they are addressing a need, and that there is money to be made. Economic niches will be filled, by fair means or foul - Americans learned that lesson back in the 1920s when the Federal Government attempted to ban the consumption of alcohol. During the thirteen years the Volstead Act was in force, an unlooked for side effect was the emergence of *'rampant underground, organised and widespread criminal activity'*[16].

People will drink, people will smoke tobacco, and people will drive around in vehicles powered by internal combustion engines, until satisfactory substitutes are found. That is the principle on which indirect taxation

---

16 http://en.wikipedia.org/wiki/Prohibition_in_the_United_States

is founded, whatever alternative rationalisations are put forward. A 17th century English poet, Henry Aldrich, wrote:

If on my theme I rightly think,
There are five reasons why men drink,
Good wine, a friend, because I 'm dry,
Or lest I should be by and by,
Or any other reason why.

Substitute '*smoke*' or '*drive cars*' for the underlined word, make one or two other necessary amendments, and the resulting epigram will be equally true. Governments know this, and see a bottomless source of revenue. Unfortunately, as with other forms of taxation, the burden tends to fall disproportionately on those at the middle and lower ends of the income spectrum. The wealthy find ways to circumvent the annoyance: company expense accounts, legal forms of tax avoidance, duty-free purchases while traveling abroad – or if the worst comes to the worst, most have plenty of slack in their disposable incomes.

In countries like Turkey, the problems are exacerbated by poverty. Turks, as has been noted, pay more than double the price for petrol that US drivers do, yet their per capita GDP is less than one quarter of that in the USA (IMF 2010 figures). And, of course, such figures represent a national average, and disguise the fact that fifty percent of the population have incomes substantially below the national average.

The bottom line, to use a phrase much beloved of businessmen and economists, is that indirect taxes hit hardest the poorest sections of the population. So what are they to do? For the most part, they won't stop drinking and smoking (even paupers need some small pleasures in life), though they may be obliged to do without private cars. Human nature being what it is, then, we can expect the following results:

- Some enterprising souls will find ways to manufacture alcoholic beverages. In Turkey, there have recently been reports of deaths related to the consumption of illegally distilled spirits. In fact last summer there was a minor scandal caused by the deaths of some Russian tourists.

- Smuggling. '*Kaçak*' is an important word in Turkish, with a multitude of meanings, but, in the case of cigarettes, for example, it has the connotation of 'unofficially duty-free'.

- The involvement of organized crime syndicates. Some reports on the deaths in Şırnak province suggest that, at the very least, PKK insurgents are taking a commission from smugglers to allow safe passage.

So, coming back to where we began, and the question of blame for the deaths of the young men from Uludere, I would suggest that inequality of income and opportunity lie at the root of the tragedy. The New Year edition of *Time* magazine has chosen '*The Protester*' as Person of the Year for 2011 – the protester to be found in Zucotti Park, New York and Tahrir Square, Cairo; in Syntagma Square, Athens, and the streets of London. Common factors in all these protests are lack of central leadership, frustration with the inability of governments to deal with manifest injustice, and a willingness to endure pain, suffering, even death, to make their message heard. One further factor is the participation of a more educated, middle class species of protester. The less educated, lower classes are likely to turn to more direct action, such as mugging and smuggling. In the end, if the privileged classes fail to address the valid grievances of their fellow citizens, they will find increasing need for draconian security measures, and not only in China and Syria.

9

Turkey and New Zealand - Border monuments

6 February 2012

Readers of my previous book may remember a piece I wrote about the Turkish dessert, ashureh. My short essay won a competition on the website *'Changing Turkey in a Changing World'*. I attempted to retain my title in their second *'Big Idea'* competition, but this time I could only manage runner-up. The topic was:

Border monuments are often designed to celebrate mobility and interconnectedness. According to the architect Cecil Balmond, "A border offers identity but one that is enriched by neighbours, so that it's not so much a line of separation as a local set of interconnected values."

We are seeking short essays (max. 1,500 words) on any European border monument. Entries are invited on these or any other border monuments located in Europe. We are particularly interested in learning why those monuments were built in the first place and how they contribute to the connection between two separate communities.

And here's my response . . .

Preamble

The question calls for a European border monument, so I should briefly explain why I am focussing on four – two of which are far from Europe. In doing so, I have in mind questions of my own: If borders are lines drawn to keep people apart, is their real existence on a map, or in the human mind? Do values connect on the ground, or in the mind? Does the uniting of people take place in a physical location – or in the mind?

✶✶

My home these days is in Istanbul, but I come from a country about as far from Turkey as it is possible to get. My hometown, Auckland, New Zealand, is seventeen thousand kilometres away. Carry on a little further, you'll cross the International Dateline into yesterday, and be on your way back. When my father's ancestors left the old country, Scotland, in June 1842, they endured a four-month sea voyage. When I board my Airbus 340-600 on 13 January, I'll be looking at a trip of thirty-one hours and twenty minutes. I will check out with Turkish Police at Atatürk Airport, and get a going-over from the NZ border people when I arrive in Auckland. In between, I will fly over half the world, mostly at an altitude of around ten thousand metres.

It is self-evident that borders these days are not as straightforward as they used to be. Turkey has an almost ten thousand kilometre-long border on land and sea – but where do customs officers do most of their business? Airports, I guess. New Zealand has fifteen thousand kilometres of coastline, and no border with another country – yet we are one of the world's most peripatetic people, constantly crossing international borders, especially to destinations in Europe, where most of us have our roots.

Not many New Zealanders have roots in Turkey. However, a surprisingly large number visit the country each year – many of them on a pilgrimage that has become an annual event towards the end of April. They flock to the town of Çanakkale, attend a solemn dawn parade with politicians and neighbours from Australia, and visit the cemeteries and killing-fields of that long-ago exercise in military futility, the Gallipoli invasion.

The first time I visited that desolate landscape was with a group from the Turkish school where I had begun working as a teacher of English. The date was 18 March, a few weeks before the latter-day Anzacs would arrive, but the day on which Turks commemorate their victory. The highlight for me was ascending to the ridge overlooking the peninsula, known to Turks as Conk Bayırı, and in Anzac legend as Chunuk Bair. This narrow strip of land was the key to the campaign, and the objective of a twelve-day battle in August 1915. Reports tell us that it was the only Allied success of the entire Gallipoli invasion – sad when you consider that a small force of New Zealanders fought their way up and held the ridge for a mere forty-eight hours, suffering horrendous losses, before being driven off by the Ottoman counter-attack.

The positive thing, from a New Zealand point-of-view is that there, on that ridge of ghosts, stand two memorials. The larger one commemorates the hero of the Ottoman defence, Colonel Mustafa Kemal, who went on to become the founder and first president of the Republic of Turkey. Alongside is a second shrine, to the memory of the young men from New Zealand who fought and died on that lonely ridge, so far from home and family. It is this latter monument on which I will focus, and to which we will return.

Seventeen thousand kilometres away, on a hillside near Wellington, the capital city of New Zealand, a site chosen for its remarkable similarity to the terrain of Gallipoli, stands another monument, this one to the memory of that same Mustafa Kemal (later Atatürk). There is no line on any map linking or separating the two countries. The distance between them is as great as possible between two places on planet Earth – yet these two monuments so far apart, represent an interconnectedness, a sharing of history and values, that transcend mere physical distance.

Young men from New Zealand and Australia, loyal citizens of the British Empire, spent a month travelling by ship to Europe, to fight for King and Country in the Great War. Thousands of them never returned, but left their remains on foreign fields. One might expect that Turks, at least, would harbour some ill-feeling against people who travelled so far with aggressive intent – but it is not so. Inscribed on that monument near Wellington are the magnanimous words of the Turkish leader:

"Those heroes that shed their blood and lost their lives . . . You are now lying in the soil of a friendly country. Therefore rest in peace. There is no difference between the Johnnies and the Mehmets to us where they lie side by side now here in this country of ours . . . You, the mothers, who sent your sons from faraway countries, wipe away your tears; your sons are now lying in our bosom and are in peace. After having lost their lives on this land they have become our sons as well."

It was in recognition of this great-heartedness, that the government of New Zealand raised a memorial to Atatürk on the ridge above Tarakena Bay, and in acknowledgment of the Turkish government's allowing the building of the NZ shrine at Chunuk Bair – commemorating the 850 Kiwi 'Johnnies' who *'lie in the bosom'* of the Turkish Republic. These two monuments link the hearts and minds of two nations whose birth pangs can be traced to those bloody months on the Gallipoli Peninsula in 1915. The words of a Turkish poet, Necmettin Halil Onan, are inscribed in huge letters on a hillside overlooking the Dardanelle Straits, and the lines could be as true for New Zealand as for Turkey:

Traveller, pause. An era ended
Where you heedless tread. Listen
And hear, in the silence of this
Mound, a nation's beating heart.[17]

---

17 My translation

But there is more to this connection. A few years ago I was wandering along Raglan Beach, on the West Coast of New Zealand's North Island, when I chanced upon three carved wooden sculptures, unmistakably Maori: a traditional tattooed male figure, a bird and a dolphin, all silver-grey and weathered by the winds and salt spray sweeping in from two thousand kilometres of one of the world's wildest seas.

Aotearoa, as the indigenous Maori people call New Zealand, is a lonely, isolated land, bordered on all sides by vast oceans, and, it goes without saying, no contiguous neighbours. Anthropologists tell us that these islands were the last habitable landmass to be populated by humans, who made their landing less than a thousand years ago. Those first arrivals, the Maori, maintained their splendid isolation for perhaps five centuries before Europeans began to arrive from the late 1700s. For the next hundred years, immigrants from Europe faced a journey of four months on a sailing ship. And there we are to this day, descendants of those intrepid pioneers, inhabiting a cluster of islands in the South Pacific Ocean, far from our roots in the British Isles, speaking a language whose closest relations are half a world away. The carved figures are not of European origin, yet they speak eloquently of our isolation, and search for identity.

I have seen a lot of Turkey, but there is a line I have yet to travel – east from the capital Ankara through the Anatolian cities of Sivas, Erzincan and Erzurum, to Kars and the Armenian border. Out there, 1,174 kilometres, and a universe away from the European metropolis of Istanbul, lies the town of Manzikert (Malazgirt in Turkish) in the province of Muş. As every Turkish school child will tell you, this was the site of a battle in 1071 CE, when the forces of the Seljuk Turkish Sultan Alparslan defeated the army of the Byzantine Emperor, Romanus Diogenes. His victory opened the way for Turks to sweep into Anatolia, where they remain today – in defiance of the feelings of many Western Europeans, who wish they would return to whence they came.

My fourth monument is there, in that remote East Anatolian town – erected in 1989 to commemorate a long ago battle. It may be debatable whether this edifice is in Europe, but the Turks indisputably are, as out of place with their language and traditions as we white New Zealanders are down there in the South Pacific. It's a strange world we live in, and sources of conflict are easy to find. The borders we draw, on the ground and in our minds, are often lines of defence. Crossing them to make connections requires imagination and breadth of vision. My four monuments can be seen as unconnected and irrelevant – or as pointers to a new world where we seek the values we share, rather than the differences that divide us.

(Word count (including Preamble) = 1495)

10

Censorship and Freedom of Speech -
How does Turkey shape up?

18 February 2012

I want to come right out and admit I haven't read any of Paul Auster's sixteen novels[18]. Sadly, it seems he is not highly esteemed by critics in his native America. I checked out reviews in *New Yorker* and elsewhere, and the overall tone was dismissive. On the other hand, he is, apparently, much read in Europe, and interestingly, is currently climbing the best-seller lists in Turkey. So it seems a pity that he has refused to visit a potential market of seventy-five million eager readers.

What attracted my attention to Mr Auster was the eruption, in the press, of a minor war of words between him and the Turkish Prime Minister. Mr Tayyip Erdoğan is quoted as having said, more or less, *"Do we care if he comes or doesn't come?"* Certainly there was no suggestion that Auster would be prevented from entering Turkey. The Leader of the Opposition has made it known that he has issued a personal invitation, and good on him, say I.

---

18 That was then – now I have, and I can tell you I enjoyed it

Still, the fact remains that Paul Auster clearly wants it on record that he is refusing to honour Turkey with a visit, and it's a matter of principle, not merely a stunt to publicise himself and increase sales of his books (which are not banned in Turkey). The problem, it seems, is that the Turkish government has been imprisoning *"journalists and writers"* in numbers, depending on who is telling the story, from forty, to a hundred, to more than a thousand.

Well, I live in the country. I read local newspapers, I watch local television and I take an interest in local affairs. If the government is truly rounding up and imprisoning journalists and writers without due process, I want to know about it. Just across Turkey's southeastern border the government of Syrian President Bashar al-Assad has resorted to shelling whole towns whose citizens have expressed discontent with the regime. The tiny island kingdom of Bahrain, on the Persian Gulf, linked to Saudi Arabia by a twenty-five-kilometre causeway, has recently suppressed its own popular uprisings with the help of tanks supplied by its equally tyrannical neighbour.

Turkey, on the other hand, has a democratically elected government. Not everyone loves the AK Party regime of Tayyip Erdoğan, however, and many of my Turkish friends, neighbours and colleagues express their dislike openly. Newspaper columnists blatantly criticise, cartoonists mock and satirise, as far as I can see, without let or hindrance. Television current affairs programmes discuss the issues of the day with seeming impunity. I have heard of no arrests or disappearances among people I know, or people known by people I know.

So who are these "writers" in custody, and why are they there? The first thing that strikes me is Auster's claim that *"nearly a hundred writers"* are imprisoned in Turkey. Well, that's a lot of writers by anyone's count. Are they full-time journalists, I wonder? Novelists? Poets? Writers of academic textbooks? Or unpublished part-time scribblers like myself? One name that often crops up is Ragip Zarakolu, so I checked him out online, and clearly he is a man with the courage of his convictions. Turkey underwent three military coups between 1960 and 1980, and Mr Zarakolu apparently upset the generals with his challenging of censorship laws relating to human rights abuses, Kurdish nationalism and the Armenian question, among other sensitive issues. In the 1970s and early 80s, he seems to have been in and out of prison, and had his passport revoked by the government of the day. Since the accession of the current AK Party government in 2003, Ragip Bey has faced several prosecutions, but has so far managed to avoid imprisonment, despite, it seems, his continued efforts to publish books and articles on issues generally accepted as requiring careful handling in Turkey.

Two other names that are attracting some sympathy within Turkey are journalists Ahmet Şık and Nedim Şener. Unlike most of the other "writers", these two are more or less mainstream. They seem to have been caught up in the net, along with other people associated with a TV channel, Oda TV, of two major related investigations, known as *Ergenekon* and *Balyoz*, that have been going on in Turkey for four or five years. It is extremely difficult to get a handle on exactly what these affairs are all about, but, as I understand, they seem to have something to do with the following:

- Some sectors of the population who like to consider themselves republican, secularist, Kemalist and nationalist, support the concept of a military takeover when the democratic process doesn't seem to be producing the results they would like.

- Groups within the Turkish military have staged three-and-a-half military coups since 1960. They suppressed left-wing dissent, while encouraging ultra-nationalist sentiment and displaying, at best, an ambivalent attitude to the Muslim religion.

- There is minority but powerful organised opposition to the popularly elected AK Party government of Tayyıp Erdoğan, using overt and clandestine methods against it rather than working through the democratic process and the ballot box.

- Mr Erdoğan's government has been working to reduce the influence of the military on the internal political affairs of the nation.

- Prior to the accession of Mr Erdoğan's government, there had been serious concern in Turkey about a concept known as *'Deep State'*, which implied some kind of unholy alliance involving high-ranking politicians, police and military personnel, business leaders and organised crime syndicates. One manifestation of this was the so-called *'Susurluk'*[19] affair, whose intricacies never seemed to be explained to public satisfaction.

- Critics from the left and right, within Turkey and without, seem to be cooperating in using issues such as Kurdish nationalism, the Armenian issue, freedom of the press and the bogey of Islamic fundamentalism to encourage opposition to the government.

In fact, it's way too much for most Turkish citizens to understand, never mind a foreigner with a limited grasp of the language. However, it's hard to live in the country for any length of time without forming some kind of opinion on these matters, and I'd like to share my thoughts with you.

Democracy is a fragile flower that needs careful nurturing. The first genuinely democratic election in Turkey was held in 1950. As has been noted, the democratic process was usurped by three military coups between 1960 and 1980. Ostensibly, government was handed back to the Turkish people in 1983, but some are of the opinion that the newly elected government was engineered by the military leaders. If you measure democracy by the ability of a country's citizens to freely elect their government, it could be argued that democracy in Turkey dates from 1997, the last time the Turkish military interfered to depose an elected government.

Fifteen years is not a long time. The United States Declaration of Independence, promulgated in 1776, asserted, among other things:

"We hold these truths to be self-evident, that all men are created equal, that they are endowed by their Creator with certain unalienable Rights, that among

---

19 http://en.wikipedia.org/wiki/Susurluk_scandal

these are Life, Liberty and the pursuit of Happiness. — That to secure these rights, Governments are instituted among Men, deriving their just powers from the consent of the governed, — That whenever any Form of Government becomes destructive of these ends, it is the Right of the People to alter or to abolish it, and to institute new Government, laying its foundation on such principles and organizing its powers in such form, as to them shall seem most likely to effect their Safety and Happiness."

At that time in US history, *"the People"* were *"men"*. It would be 164 years before women were given the constitutional right *"to alter or abolish"* governments. African Americans were definitely not *"People"*, since the practice of slavery continued until the 13th Amendment abolished it in 1865. I'm not even going to mention the Native Americans' situation, but it must be fair to say that legal and socially sanctioned racial segregation continued for much of the 20th century.

Clearly, democracy is a controversial term in itself. How do you measure it? Elsewhere I have noted the tendency of undemocratic regimes to make liberal use of the term. The right to vote is generally cited as an important cornerstone of the democratic process, but how much power does that really give us? Emma Goldman, once described as *'the most dangerous woman in America'*, is reputed to have said: *"If voting changed anything, they'd make it illegal"*. Cynical, you'd have to say, especially since she lived from 1869 to 1940. But sometimes you wonder, don't you? I can't find who first came up with the pithy aphorism: *"America has the best democracy money can buy"*, but look at the facts. Lobbying is a multi-million dollar industry in the US. Wall St and the financial industry spent hundreds of million of dollars on lobbyists influencing lawmakers to deregulate their industry so that they could fleece investors, fill their own pockets and undermine the entire US economy. Elected representatives move out of Congress and into highly paid jobs using their 'insider' knowledge and contacts on behalf of wealthy clients in the lobbying industry. In short, if you can't afford to lobby, forget democracy.

I don't want to go into the matter here – anyway, I have touched on it in a previous chapter – but it could be argued that, at least beyond their own shores, governments in the United States tend to prefer autocratic, dictatorial regimes. On the whole, it is easier and more straightforward to deal with governments that don't have to take into account the fickle opinions of an enfranchised electorate.

But I'm getting away from Turkey here, and the issue we started with, which is freedom of speech, or more specifically freedom of the press. Ideally it's desirable that writers should be free to express themselves, politically or artistically, without fear of harassment or imprisonment. Undoubtedly, in Turkey, that is not always the case, while the US situation has apparently improved since the "Dubya" Bush administration passed into history. However, it's not a clear-cut issue. Obviously there are areas where other factors take precedence over freedom of speech: incitement to crime, child pornography, defamation, and national security, to name a few. Turks, for example, have fallen victim to curtailment of freedom with the French Government's recent decision to prevent them from defending themselves against accusations of genocide against Armenians.

As we noted above, democratic freedoms in Turkey are not as well established as in most Western democracies. Turkey as a nation came into being in 1923 after the disintegration of the Ottoman Empire. Its founding principle, Turkish nationalism, was a new concept that had to be introduced and established in order to create a viable state. In the cauldron of war and political and economic upheaval, undoubtedly myths were invented and half-truths disseminated. Minority rights were overlooked or shelved, as in all national struggles, in the interests of unity. It is only in recent years, perhaps the last decade, that Turks have come to feel confident enough in their own identity that they can permit discussion of issues such as, for example, the Kurdish question, and the place of religion in a secular state. That these issues can now be discussed openly is a measure of an increasing maturity of Turkish society.

Paul Auster is, of course, entitled to his opinion about Turkey – though one might have hoped that an open-minded writer would want to visit the country and form his own opinions, rather than rely on those of others. He refers, for example, to the international organization *PEN*, formed in

1921 *"to promote friendship and intellectual co-operation among writers everywhere"*. When you check their website, you can't escape the feeling that literary aims have taken a back seat these days to a political agenda. That's their right, too, certainly, and their aims may be very worthy, but perhaps they should consider changing their name so that it gives a more honest indication of their raison d'etre.

One similar organization which does that, is *Reporters Without Borders (RSF)*. They publish an index each year indicating how they rate countries in terms of journalistic freedom. They are unabashedly a political organization, though, again, their name is a little deceptive. Clearly it was intended to reflect a similarity of purpose to *Doctors Without Borders (MSF)*, whose members give assistance to people in countries whose own governments, for whatever reason, are unable to do so. While the very presence of MSF doctors in a country may imply failures on the part of that country's government, for the most part, they seem to refrain from making political judgments.

Still, the world of art is in a different universe, and artists are jealous of their freedom to express. Another writer who has been in trouble in Turkish courts is the novelist Orhan Pamuk. Pamuk was awarded the Nobel Prize for Literature in 2006, though he is not well loved, nor, as far as I can learn, much read in his own country (at least in the books that won him the big prize). I worked my way through one-and-a-half novels from his prize-winning canon, albeit in translation, and I have to confess I found them barely readable – though that may not always be a disadvantage when it comes to winning literary awards. A more positive advantage may be the expressing of political views that do not endear the writer to his own government. Pamuk was charged under Turkish Law with insulting the Turkish Republic, for suggesting that Turks were responsible for the mass killing of Kurds and Armenians. Interestingly, the charges were subsequently dropped, and the lawyer instrumental in instigating the case, has been arrested as a player in the *Ergenekon* investigation discussed above.

Well, that's a good sign, for sure. Whatever you may think about Pamuk as a giant of literature, you can't say he really deserves to be locked up. And if the aforesaid lawyer turns out to have been an ultra-nationalist right-wing fanatic making death threats against well-meaning novelists, then justice in Turkey may have turned the corner. On the other hand, there are those in the country who hold that *Ergenekon* is a fictitious creation of the AK Party government to silence opposition. Another journalist, Tuncay Özkan, arrested in the round-up, recently appealed against his arrest to the European Court of Human Rights. Perhaps surprisingly, the European Court rejected Özkan's complaint, and defined *Ergenekon* as a *"terrorist organization attempting to topple the government by the use of force."*

So, what do you make of all that? As that great comic genius Spike Milligan used to say, *"It's all rather confusing, really."* As an outsider, I am not really competent to make a definitive statement, but what I can say is this. Unlike Paul Auster, I came to Turkey. I live here, and have formed my own opinions about the country and its people. If Mr Auster comes, I can take him to easily accessible bookshops where he can purchase reading matter on all the controversial issues, from Kurdish nationalism to the Assyrian 'genocide'. I can show him ample evidence of a healthy press sounding off against the ruling government, seemingly without fear of imprisonment and torture. He can watch (with a little assistance) current affairs programmes on several television channels discussing all the questions of the day. And no doubt he'll be happy to see his own novels climbing the local best-seller lists.

11

Armenian Massacres and the Nationalism of Hate

4 March 2012

A large crowd gathered in Taksim Square, Istanbul, on Saturday 25 February to commemorate the 20th anniversary of an event they were calling the Khojaly Massacre. Evidently there were some unruly elements, and among the placards there were a few thinly veiled threats against Armenians and locals who might be inclined to sympathise with them. A little unpleasant, but you get that kind of stuff at any demonstration, right?

Still, you'd have to be curious about the event, wouldn't you – the Khojaly Massacre? What's that all about? Well, I can tell you, the incident occurred back in 1993 during the local war that had broken out between neighbouring states, Armenia and Azerbaijan, over the disputed territory of Nagorno-Karabakh. The problem apparently was/is that, despite being located within the borders of Azerbaijan, the area has a majority Armenian population, which provided the Armenian government with a pretext for sending in troops and annexing it.

Unfortunately, as in any war, the casualties included not a few civilians, and the bloodiest incident took place in or around the town of Khojaly.

Needless to say, accounts vary according to whether you're listening to the Armenian or the Azeri side of the story – how many women and children were slaughtered, how it was done, and what was done to them beforehand. Anyway, to cut a long story short, Nagorno-Karabakh became a pseudo-independent state sponsored by Armenia, and the Azeris remain pretty unhappy about it.

Now, you may or may not know that Turkey and Azerbaijan have a kind of big brother-little brother relationship. Azeris speak a Ural-Altaic language that is the nearest relative in the world to Turkish. If you speak Turkish, you can watch Azeri television, get a few patronising laughs, and understand about sixty to seventy percent of what they're talking about. Accordingly, in a show of solidarity with their smaller sibling, the Turkish government closed the border they share with Armenia. 'So what?' you may think. Armenians don't love Turks that much. They're probably happy to have a closed border. But take a look at a map. Armenia is a tiny, land-locked country, surrounded by some pretty shady, even dangerous, neighbours. Ironically, Turkey is probably the least threatening among them, and certainly provides the most stable and direct route to the west for goods and people travelling in and out of Armenia.

In the last two or three years, the Turkish government has indicated a readiness to engage in negotiations with their Armenian neighbours, with a view to reopening the border. However, they are insisting on the need for a fair and reasonable settlement of the Nagorno-Karabakh issue – and that the Armenians back off a little on their 'genocide' claims. Surprisingly, as far as the actual nation of Armenia is concerned, the latter issue is less of a problem than the former. Most of the noise about an alleged Armenian holocaust originates in the diaspora. Local Armenians seem much more inclined to employ the soft pedal. Gwynne Dyer[20], a historian and journalist who has made a study of the issues has this to say:

For Armenians abroad, making the Turks admit that they planned and carried out a genocide is supremely important. Indeed, it has become a core part of

20 http://www.straight.com/article-264662/gwynne-dyer-ending-debate-armenian-genocide

72

their identity. For most of those who are still in Armenia, getting the Turkish border re-opened is a higher priority. Their poverty and isolation are so great that a quarter of the population has emigrated since the border was closed [in 1993], *and trade with their relatively rich neighbour to the west would help to staunch the flow.*

Vartan Harutiunian a writer and human rights activist in Armenia, and political prisoner in the days when Armenia was part of the Soviet empire, has suggested that self-pity and anti-Turkism lie at the heart of Armenian nationalism. *'The most patriotic Armenian',* he says, *'is the most anti-Turkish'.*

Christopher Sisserian, a freelance journalist and graduate student of International Politics at the School of Oriental and African Studies (SOAS), London, has recently published an article entitled *'Understanding the Importance of a Shared History*[21]. He argues that:

'The separation of Armenians and Turks in 1915 is a comparatively recent phenomenon. In order for an understanding to be reached between the two nations regarding the genocide of 1915, it is first necessary to re-discover the history of two peoples living side by side harmoniously for hundreds of years . . . An understanding of this is the first step in re-humanising the relations between the two nations and promoting reconciliation. Armenians and Turks have dehumanized each other, often understandably, in the process of maintaining their separate cultural identities. Armenians learning about the genocide are led to believe all Turks were (and by extension still are) inherently evil, ignoring the many Turks that endeavored to save Armenian lives. Correspondingly, Turks alive today who bear no responsibility for the events of 1915 are incensed by accusations that they are guilty of a crime not committed by them.'

There's a tone of calm, balanced reason there, don't you think, that is not commonly heard when this issue is discussed? Nationalism has been

---

21 http://www.opendemocracy.net/christopher-sisserian/understanding-importance-of-shared-history

a two-headed monster since it surfaced as a rationale for political action towards the end of the 18th century. Unscrupulous seekers of power have been all too ready to unleash its forces of unity and aggression to further their own ends. Anatolia and the Balkan lands have been traversed and conquered by so many races and peoples since time immemorial that it is impossible to know who were the aboriginal inhabitants. The search for racial and national purity is futile, yet the very diversity of ethnic and linguistic groups drives a powerful need for identity.

One admission can be readily made. The ancestors of today's Armenians have been in Anatolia longer than Turks – but relativity is an important factor here. The Seljuk Turks won the victory that allowed them entry into Anatolia[22] around the same time that the Normans defeated the Anglo-Saxons, and asserted their right to rule England. It would be no easy task these days to separate out the descendants of the Norman invaders and send them back to France.

Even if we accept that the invading Turks rode roughshod over the democratic rights of those who controlled Anatolia at the time, it was the Byzantine Greeks, not the Armenians who were in charge. As far as I can discover, there was a Kingdom of Armenia in ancient times, experiencing a brief Golden Age between 95 and 66 BCE under the rule of Tigranes the Great. Centuries later, there was a period of independence between 884 and 1045 CE, when the Bagratuni dynasty ruled from their capital city of Ani, now an uninhabited ruin located in Eastern Turkey. Apart from those interludes, Armenians have been a conquered people, ruled successively by Assyrians, Greeks, Romans, Byzantines, Arabs, Mongols, Persians, Ottomans and Russians (Imperial and Soviet). Some historians argue that the Ottomans were the kindest and most tolerant of these masters, allowing cultural, religious, linguistic and economic freedom to a privileged people within their imperial borders.

Nevertheless, being a minority people within a dominant culture is not an easy condition to bear. There will always be voices saying that

---

22 The Battle of Manzikert/Malazgırt, 1071 CE

independence and autonomy would bring greater happiness – and who is to say they are wrong? The artist, Mkrtum Hovnatanian (1779-1846), was among the first to foster a consciousness of Armenian traditions and history through his paintings. Mikayel Chamchian, imperial jeweller to the Ottoman Sultan in Istanbul, wrote a grammar of the Armenian language, and a history of the Armenian people, towards the end of the 18th century. A religious leader and writer, Khrimian Hayrik (Migirdiç Hirimyan), worked to improve the lot of Armenian peasants in eastern Anatolia from the 1860s, and argued for self-determination. Interestingly, he served in Istanbul as Armenian Patriarch for a time, recognised by the Ottoman government, while his appeal to the Berlin Conference in 1878 for European support for Armenian self-determination apparently fell on deaf ears.

From the early 19th century, the Russian Empire fought several wars against Persians and Ottomans, with the aim, as ever, of forging a corridor for themselves to the warm waters of the Black Sea and the Mediterranean. To further this aim, it suited them to encourage Armenians in a belief that they had common interests as fellow Christians. Armenians fought on the side of the Russians in the 1820s, and again in the 1870s. In the mid-19th century, Britain and France opposed Russian expansion, and even went to war against them, in support of the Ottomans[23]. Later, however, as Russian chauvinism increased from the 1880s, the Tsarist government began to crack down on Armenian nationalism, closing schools and discouraging use of the language. It was at this point in history that Armenian revolutionary movements really began to grow, encouraged by the British, who suddenly started to take an interest in their 'fellow Christians'. The part played by the increasing importance of petroleum in Western economies could make an interesting study, which I do not, however, intend to pursue here.

Suffice it to say that the activities of British and American 'missionaries' increased towards the end of the 19th century, in parts of Ottoman Anatolia where many Armenians lived, and subsequently revolts broke out against the Ottoman government. You might want to ask why missionaries

---

23 The Crimean War: 1853-6

were necessary when the Armenians were already Christian, but let's leave that aside as well. From the 1870s, revolutionary Armenian groups such as the *Hunchaks* and *Dashnaks* began to incite and carry out acts of violence. Undoubtedly, something very dreadful befell Armenian people in Anatolia in 1915 – but balanced histories acknowledge that Armenians were not alone in their suffering. Justin McCarthy professor of history at Louisville University, Kentucky, has written much on the subject.

What seems clear is that there has been, at the very least, a one-sided presentation of a very complex story, to the severe detriment of Turkey's international reputation. In 1919, shortly after the Armenian tragedy of 1915, Holly-wood produced a film, black and white and silent of course, purporting to tell the story of a young Armenian woman who had escaped after horrific experiences in Turkish harems and slave-markets. Stills from this salacious film, *'Ravished Armenians'*, occasionally turn up in literature arguing for recognition of a genocide.

A name that also comes up in this literature is Henry Morgenthau. This gentleman was US ambassador to the Ottoman Empire from 1913-1916. Morgenthau was no lover of the Ottomans, and reportedly went somewhat unwillingly to the post. Despite the fact that he was domiciled in Istanbul, and did not visit the troubled areas, preferring to rely on reports for his information, he is frequently quoted from his own writings on Ottoman atrocities. Interestingly, one of Morgenthau's successors, Admiral Mark Bristol, US High Commissioner to the Ottoman Empire (and later Turkey) from 1919 to 1927, who did take the trouble to visit the area and speak to eyewitnesses, is generally ignored by genocide proponents, probably because he presents a more balanced picture of events. Bristol worked hard to get recognition in the USA for the new Republic of Turkey, and argued:

'The new regime in Turkey is a most remarkable evidence of a revolution in form and administration of a government. Briefly, an absolute monarchy has been re-placed by a republic. Church has been separated from state and religion eliminated from all law codes. Religion of any kind may be taught in the churches and the mosques, but not in the schools. All persons born in Turkey, without regard to race, religion or nationality, have all rights of Turkish

citizenship. The Turkish leaders without previous experience must evolve the new administration. There are bound to be mistakes and the evolution will be slow, but there are many evidences of progress'.

An event sometimes cited in anti-Turkish propaganda is the Turkish (more properly *Ottoman*) Courts Martial of 1919-20. The courts were convened to bring to justice, perpetrators of Ottoman atrocities carried out on Armenians and others. One or two convictions resulted in executions, but most of the charges were eventually dropped. It should not be forgotten that Istanbul was under occupation by British forces at the time, and the Ottoman Sultan with his government were puppets eager to absolve themselves of guilt, to find scapegoats, and to curry favour with the occupying powers.

Between 1973 and 1994, Armenian terrorist organisations (or nationalist activists, if you prefer), such as ASALA[24], carried out attacks on consulates and embassies in several European and US cities, resulting in the deaths of forty-two Turkish diplomats and four foreign nationals. Fifteen Turks and sixty-six foreign nationals were injured in these incidents. The stated aim was to raise world awareness and support for labelling as genocide the events of 1915.

Writers such as Vahakn Dadrian, Taner Akçam and Richard Hovanissian continue to turn out publications attacking Turkey and demanding the recognition of an Armenian Genocide, despite having been caught out on numerous counts of mistranslation of documents, selective reporting, and misrepresentation of facts.

Most recently, the French government of Nicholas Sarkozy has been trying to proscribe attempts to counter accusations of genocide against Turkey. Striking a blow for justice and democracy, the French Constitutional Council have apparently rejected the draft law as unconstitutional, obliging the French President to return to the drawing-board and reconsider his vote-catching exercise.

---

24 http://www.armenians.com/asala/index1.html

The Pandora jar of nationalist ideology was opened more than two centuries ago, and it is way too late now to re-stopper it. Politicians and power-seekers in Turkey and Armenia, in Europe and the Balkans, even in the United States of America, are only too willing to enlist the support of the ignorant and disaffected by employing nationalist rhetoric to arouse hatred and instigate violence against a stereotyped enemy. Organised demonstrations such as the one in Taksim Square serve only to stir up nationalistic fervour and focus aggression. All that remains in the ideological jar is hope – the hope that voices of reason and moderation will prevail, and past wrongs can be forgiven and forgotten. The alternative is too awful to contemplate.

The Circassian Genocide - I'm a Caucasian too!

16 May 2012

I was out and about last Sunday, showing a couple of friends from New Zealand around various parts of the city, and my eye was drawn to posters on a subway wall in Karaköy. The text was in Turkish, of course, so it meant little to my visitors, but it was announcing a demonstration planned for 21 May to commemorate the 148th anniversary of the *'Circassian Genocide'*. Participants will apparently congregate in the big square of Taksim, whence they will march down Istiklal Avenue to the Russian Consulate. There, no doubt, they intend to request politely that Vladimir Putin and his government apologise, and perhaps make some restitution for the displacement, deaths and expropriations that took place in the years leading up to that date in 1864.

I did mention this matter briefly in an earlier chapter, but I have to confess, I wasn't aware at that stage of the full ramifications. Well, I wouldn't presume to claim even now that I've got everything worked out, but it's an interesting business for sure, and its effects are still being felt in a part of the world most of us have heard of – though we might have trouble locating it on a map. Anyway, let's plunge in and see where we end up.

First of all, I'm not much of an expert on Russian history, so I did what I usually do when I feel the need to improve an area of weakness – I 'googled' 'Russian Empire' and read a few of the suggested sources. Interestingly, none of them made any mention of invading or conquering the Caucasus or Crimean regions. The nearest they came was references to several wars with the Ottoman Empire as a result of which territory was gained and the Empire was expanded southwards.

Now, you can't really blame the Russians for wanting to expand south and west. I'm sure Russia is a lovely country, but it's not blessed with harbours and access to warm water seas. Accordingly, in the 18th century, Tsar Peter the Great succeeded in wresting access to the Baltic from Sweden and established his new capital, St Petersburg. Another Russian 'Great' by the name of Catherine continued the drive south towards the Black Sea, and here, it seems, lie the roots of our problem with the Circassians. Most of the Ottoman imperial expansion had been completed a hundred years earlier, and undoubtedly not all of the conquered peoples were totally happy with the new situation. Nevertheless, the Ottomans did allow certain freedoms to their subjects, among them, freedom of language and religion. The Russians, on the other hand, were evidently somewhat less accommodating. Lands in the path of their southward expansion were populated largely by Muslims with distinct languages and cultures, and clearly this was not in keeping with the grand plan of a Russian-speaking, Orthodox Christian empire.

I don't want to get sidetracked from my main subject, but the first people to suffer from the Russians' grand plan were the Crimean Tatars. Crimea had been part of the Ottoman dominions since the 15th century, and its inhabitants were mostly Turkic speaking Muslims. After the Russians' military defeat of the Ottomans in the 1770s, they proceeded to annex Crimea and colonise it with Christian Slavs. It has been estimated that, over the next century, two-thirds of the Tatar population abandoned their homes and emigrated to various parts of the Ottoman Empire, many of them perishing on the way.

We may imagine that word of this had reached the Tatars' near neighbours in the Caucasus area, and when they saw signs that the Russians were aiming to move in their direction, they decided to resist. Some resistance they put up, in fact! The Caucasus War, also known as the Russian conquest of the Caucasus, lasted from 1817 until 1864 (the year referred to on those posters we mentioned above). The Circassians were the most organised, most determined and most militarily capable of the Caucasian peoples and their struggle bore the brunt of the Russian invasion. These people, who call themselves Adyghe, are considered to be the indigenous natives of the Caucasus region. In fact their resistance was such that the Russians were unable to subdue them by force of arms alone. The preferred method became a policy of clearance – burning of villages and killing or driving out the Muslim inhabitants. The author, Leo Tolstoy, served with the Russian army in the Caucasus, and the experience seems to have been the catalyst that turned him from a life of wealthy idleness to one of creativity, spirituality, pacifism and renunciation of privilege. One of his quoted observations:

"It had been the custom to rush the auls [mountain villages] by night, when, taken by surprise, the women and children had no time to escape, and the horrors that ensued under the cover of darkness when the Russian soldiers made their way by twos and threes into the houses were such as no official narrator dared describe."

Another contemporary observer, a British consul by the name of Dickson, also reported: *"A Russian detachment captured the village of Toobah on the Soobashi river, inhabited by about a hundred Abadzekh [a tribe of Circassians], and after these had surrendered themselves prisoners, they were all massacred by the Russian Troops. Among the victims were two women in an advanced state of pregnancy and five children.*

At such a distance of time it is not possible to arrive at an absolute figure for the death toll. Some Circassian historians claim a figure of four million; official Russian reports say perhaps three hundred thousand. Less partisan sources suggest somewhere around a million and a half.

Undoubtedly, apart from those killed during the war itself, huge numbers perished as a result of forced migration. Thousands died of hunger and disease after being driven from their villages; thousands more on the Black Sea beaches as they waited for Ottoman ships to ferry them away. More still were drowned when overcrowded vessels sank in passage, and more again after reaching the sanctuary of Ottoman territory in the insanitary conditions that prevailed there. The land, dwellings and possessions they left behind were taken over by Russians, Ukrainians, Armenians, Cossacks and Georgians, brought in to repopulate and 'Christianise' the area. Once again, we may imagine the feelings of anger and resentment these events stirred up, not only in the survivors and refugees themselves, but in the people of the Ottoman areas who listened to their tales of atrocities and suffering, and had to provide for them.

Who else knew what was going on in the Caucasus? Why do we know so little about it? These are pertinent questions. I came across an interesting source while researching this issue: an archive in the National Library of New Zealand, of a newspaper called *The NZ Spectator and Cook's Strait Guardian*. In the edition of 17 August 1864, was an article reprinted from the *London Times* of May 9, based on a report dated 28 April, from Constantinople (Istanbul):

"Official information has been received here of the capitulation of Vardar, the last stronghold of the Circassians, and of the consequent submission of all the tribes. I had occasion in a previous letter to refer to the flood of immigration which was pouring into the Turkish dominions from the Caucasus, and to the defeats which had been experienced by these gallant mountaineers; and although there could be no doubt at that time that the cause of the Circassians was hopeless, there was not sufficient ground for anticipating the extraordinary movement which has since developed itself, and which threatens, unless immediate relief and succour be obtained, to degenerate, as regards these poor people, into an awful disaster. Whether this movement is to be attributed to a panic consequent on defeat, or to the hatred inspired by the Russians, it is rather difficult to determine; but there is no doubt that the three tribes known

as the 'Shabsoukhs', Oboukhs' and 'Abazehs' have determined to abandon their country to a man, and take refuge in Turkish territory. Already the outflowing tide of emigrants is so great as to place the Turkish Government in the greatest embarrassment. 27,000 of these unfortunate creatures, in the most utter destitution, have poured into Trebizond (Trabzon). *The privations of the voyage in a most inclement season have produced disease of the very worst kind among them, which is not only committing fearful ravages in their own famished ranks, but it is extending to the local population. Typhus and smallpox are raging at Trebizond, and the place is threatened with a famine. The Turkish government is willing and anxious to receive the fugitives, and incorporate them into its own population, but the movement has been so sudden and so extensive that it has been impossible to make provision for the hosts that are daily pouring in. It is calculated that no less than 300,000 will, in the next two to three months, seek shelter in this country . . ."*

The British Ambassador to the Ottoman Empire, Sir Henry Bulwer, presented reports to the Prime Minister of the day, Earl Russell. In one such report, dated April 12, 1864, he said:

"The continued advances of the Russians in Circassia, and the ill-treatment experienced by the natives from the Russian troops, have led to an almost complete emigration from the country: 25,000 have already reached Trebizond, and others are attempting to escape in small boats at every risk. The conglomeration of vast quantities of these people, who have no industrial habits, threatens the health and peace of any one locality, and the loss of life which is occasioned by their hazardous attempts to escape from their conquerors is shocking to humanity. The Turkish Government is therefore about sending vessels to Trebizond to remove the emigrants thence, and place them in different parts of the Empire; and it is also in negotiation with the Russian Chargé d'Affaires here, in order to be able to adopt some measures by which those unfortunate people who, after the most heroic attempts in defending the country where they were born, are at last obliged to abandon it, may be able to seek an asylum with safety in the Ottoman dominions."

It seems reasonably clear, then, that the British Government of the day, and the literate public of remote New Zealand were aware of the events unfolding in the Caucasus region. Perhaps we can excuse their lack of action to alleviate the suffering of the Circassians, or to exert diplomatic pressure on the Russians. White settlers in New Zealand in those years were also engaged in forcefully driving the indigenous Maori people from their land, and suppressing their attempts to defend their way of life. The United States government was doing the same to its Native Americans, and the Redcoats of the British Empire were here, there and everywhere demonstrating to local peoples that resistance to the civilising benefits of empire was useless. It was a scant six years since the Brits had brutally put down what they liked to refer to as *'The Indian Mutiny'*. In the circumstances, it would have been difficult to act self-righteously.

Why we have 'forgotten' the Russians' treatment of the Circassians is less easy to explain, when we seem well able to 'remember' the Greeks and the Armenians. Could it be that we find it easier to attribute brutality to Muslims than to Christians? Or perhaps Armenians were better able to draw attention to their cause by the use of terror tactics. Who knows? Whatever the case, Russian ethnic cleansing of its Muslim subjects did not end in 1864. In 1943 and 1944, Josef Stalin forcefully 'relocated' hundreds of thousands from the Caucasus and Crimea to remote and desolate parts of the Soviet Union, Siberia, Kazakhstan and elsewhere in Central Asia, resulting in untold deaths.

Those Circassian demonstrators in Taksim on 21 May will be commemorating the 148th anniversary of their final defeat by the Russians – but the legacy of those days continues well into the 21st century. The population of modern Chechnya is ninety-four percent Sunni Muslim, and their struggle for independence continues. In neighbouring Dagestan, Ingushetia and North Ossetia, the situation is similar. It is unlikely, however, that Mother Russia will let her Caucasian children go, taking their wealth of oil, natural gas and other minerals with them. It is equally unlikely that President Putin will apologise to the Circassians and offer restitution for their past sufferings. After all, it was pre-Revolutionary Tsarist Russia that did the deed.

13

Who's Going to Rule the World?
Fethullah Gülen?

19 June 2012

For much of my longish life I have been hearing tales, historical, contemporary and fictional, about the latest megalomaniac individual or evil empire determined to rule the world. Traditionally the contenders have based their claims on the possession of some kind of superior weapons technology – but times have changed. We are well into the post-modern era, and most predictions of earlier ages about what the world would be like in the year 1984 or 2000 seem naïve and laughable to us now. It is pretty clear that the task of ruling the world has moved way beyond the power of one individual (if that was ever a realistic possibility). The vast military resources of the one remaining global super-power have proved insufficient to rebuild even minor third world states in the US's own image. So now we have nothing to worry about, right? We can get on with the job of lighting up our own small corners with *iPhone 4s* and *Galaxy SIIIs* without fear of global annihilation.

Uh-uh, sorry folks. I've got bad news. There's a new battle shaping up, and it's about the enemies within.

One reason I enjoy living in Turkey is that I don't feel so much like crying when I read the local news. Back in New Zealand, before heading to work, I used to listen to a morning roundup on the radio of what 'they' were doing to my beautiful country. I confess, there was a time back then when the idea of joining some revolutionary band of bomb-throwing anarchists began to have some appeal. Now, however, from a distance of some seventeen thousand kilometres, I find I can read news of events in the *Land of the Long White Cloud* with more objectivity, and the tears don't flow as once they did.

Let me give you an example of the madness, though, from my own field of professional interest. The National (read *Tory*) Government in New Zealand, in its 2012 budget, announced its intention to save $43 million by putting the lid on teacher recruitment. The inevitable result of this, of course, would be a steady increase in class sizes in schools around the country. Luckily, the government has a select band of tame 'education experts' who can be called upon to explain why this won't be a bad thing. One of these, a Professor John Hattie, has apparently conducted research showing that class sizes are not a major factor in student learning. As far as I can learn, Professor Hattie's research has not involved any actual time spent teaching actual kids in actual classrooms – he has been an ivory tower academic since 1975. Not sure I would take my car to be repaired by an 'automotive expert' with no hands-on experience, regardless of how many years he'd been studying the theory, but that's just me.

Well, there are experts and consultants, it seems, and you can count on these guys to back each other up. One of the latter, a Dr John Langley, was quoted as saying, *'If I had a choice of putting my child into a class with a poor teacher with twenty kids or into a class of thirty kids with a good teacher I'd go for the latter. It's as simple as that.'* Reassuring to know the government has access to people with such incisive problem-solving ability, and New Zealand taxpayers can feel satisfied that Dr John well deserves his no doubt generous consultancy fee.

These days New Zealand has a system of proportional system for electing representatives to its legislative assembly. The system was instituted in 1996 in response to overwhelming public dissatisfaction with the old first-past-the-post, two-party system such as exists in the UK and the US.

Unfortunately post-modernism has insinuated its way in here too. The several small parties that manage to win the occasional seat in the legislature are run mostly by fringe lunatic refugees from the far right or left of the two main parties. The main role of these minor participants seems to be putting forward outrageous proposals which the government can proceed to implement in slightly modified form after the initial public anger has died down.

One of the more fanatical of these minor political groupings is a coterie of doctrinaire libertarians known by the acronym ACT, arguing with religious fervour for deregulation, privatisation, flexible labour markets and reduced taxes for the wealthy. And one of the more significant achievements of these neo-liberal economic geniuses has been the move to privatisation of the prison system. A recent editorial[25] in the *New Zealand Herald* observed that, '*Something is clearly awry when a Government proclaims the economic benefits of a new prison*'. Nevertheless, Auckland's oldest prison has already been outsourced to private management, and a newly built facility soon will be. The group to which the NZ Government is entrusting the care and security of its criminals is a multi-national outfit name of *Serco* – which a *Guardian* journalist[26] has described as '*. . . probably the biggest company you've never heard of.*' OK, come on, you may say. Leave aside your left-wing socialist prejudices and tell us how they are doing. Well, a recent report[27] on the first eight months of Serco's management produced the following findings:

'*. . . as well as two prisoners being wrongfully released, the British firm had failed to meet 40% of its performance targets and was fined $150,000 after a prisoner escaped.*

Targets for random drug testing and prisoner management plans were also not reached.

---

25 http://www.nzherald.co.nz/nz/news/article.cfm?c_id=1&objectid=10658577

26 http://www.guardian.co.uk/business/2006/feb/24/columnists.guardiancolumnists

27 http://tvnz.co.nz/national-news/private-prison-operator-failing-meet-targets-4855095

Annually, Serco can earn up to approximately $3 million in incentive pay-
ments, but instead it is having to pay for under-performing.
On top of the $150,000 fine it got after prisoner A. F. escaped, it was fined
$25,000 for accidently releasing an inmate early and $50,000 for failing to
file progress reports.
Another $25,000 fine is pending for releasing another prisoner early.'

In spite of these criticisms, the government is standing by its decision.
Corrections Minister Anne Tolley said '. . . *there needs to be some improve-*
ment, but she also described it as a "bedding in" period for Serco'.

Well, once you have accepted handing over prisons to the private sector
you have pretty much overcome, or chosen to ignore, all the arguments
that can be mustered against privatization. So it is hardly surprising to
see the free-marketeers turning their attention to schools and teachers.
Unfortunately, private sector education has been around for a long time,
and has often been associated with elitism, poor teaching, violence, and
dubious educational standards. But even supposing they do find a good establishment, the wealthy resent having to fork out high tuition fees in addition to paying taxes, some of which are used to finance state-sector schools.
So, our privateers have come up with a system which allows organisations
to receive government funding for a school, while at the same time getting
a special deal allowing them to avoid much of the normal regulation and
overseeing. It's called the Charter School system.

However, again unfortunately, there seem to be glitches in the system.
In 2009, the Center for Research on Education Outcomes (CREDO) at
Stanford University in the US, produced a report stating that '*17% of charter*
schools reported academic gains that were significantly better than traditional
public schools; 46% showed no difference from public schools; and 37% were
significantly worse than their traditional public school counterparts'.

Now, if you have read this far, you may be wondering what all this
has to do with my topic, which, you will remember, was '*Who's going to*
rule the world?' But I assure you, I hadn't forgotten. I want to redirect your
attention to those figures in the CREDO report, and in particular, the '*17%*
of charter schools [reporting] *academic gains that were significantly better than*

traditional public schools. A Turkish colleague of mine recently sent me the link to a *'60 Minutes'* documentary[28] looking into the connection between some very successful charter schools in Texas, and a certain reclusive expatriate Turkish citizen by the name of Fethullah Gülen.

I watched the documentary with interest, because I have been hearing this gentleman's name in Turkey for some years, generally spoken in tones of fear and loathing that suggest some kind of hybrid monster cloned from the DNA of L Ron Hubbard, Sun Myung Moon, Attila the Hun and the Ayatollah Khomeini. I was hoping for some conclusive evidence of evil-doing, since I was assured that Americans were now seeing Fethullah Hodja in his true colours. The programme, then, I have to say, turned out to be something of a letdown. The presenter, a long-serving correspondent for CBS with a big reputation as an investigative tele-journalist, visited schools supposedly associated with the Gülen 'movement', and tracked the elderly Hodja to his secluded residence in the Poconos, a mountainous region in north-eastern Pennsylvania.

She and her camera crew spoke to school administrators and students. As far as I could see, they learned that:

- The school administrators are normal looking, secular and articulate.

- The students are bright-eyed, bushy-tailed kids who love their school.

- The schools are among the most highly rated in the country in terms of academic success.

- There is a waiting list for entry exceeding the total capacity of the schools.

---

28 http://www.cbsnews.com/video/watch/?id=7408418n

- There is no religious education taking place, and certainly no observable Islamic character.

- Curriculum focus is on mathematics and science.

They were unable to interview the Hodja himself since, apparently, he has been ill for some months and rarely appears in public. His representative assured the interviewer that he takes no direct interest in the running of the schools. The most sinister information emerging from the programme was the presenter's comment that some people in Turkey believe Gülen and his 'movement' have a *'secret agenda'* though the details weren't made clear – one assumes that's because otherwise it wouldn't be secret.

Undoubtedly the activities of the *'Gülen movement'* are beginning to arouse interest beyond the shores of the Hodja's native Turkey – however there seems to be some debate about the nature of these activities.

My *Apple Desktop Dictionary* defines a movement as: *'a group of people working together to advance their shared political, social, or artistic ideas: the labor movement'*, or the cubist movement.
Merriam-Webster Online suggests: *'a series of organized activities working toward an objective; also: an organized effort to promote or attain an end, eg the civil rights movement'*.

Two questions seem to arise here: Does a 'movement' require a leader in the sense of a person who takes responsibility for organizing and coordinating its activities? And, is a 'movement' good or bad, according to the definition?

Addressing the first question, it seems to me that the key factor in a movement is a concept or philosophy, rather than a 'leader' in the normal sense of the word – a concept such as: that labour needs to organize to counteract the power of employers; that human beings deserve equal rights before the law regardless of race; the use of *'multiple perspective and complex planar faceting for expressive effect'* in a work of art. Participants latch on to an idea formulated by an initiator or trendsetter and the movement takes on a life of its own which may be quite independent of that person. Subsequently leaders may emerge but again, the movement continues or dies out more or less regardless of the existence or activities of those persons. Think of Martin Luther King or Pablo Picasso. As for the second question, in general, movements tend to be, to a greater or lesser extent, revolutionary, in the sense that they are usually a reaction to the prevailing status quo, and their appeal is that they offer some kind of new approach to what is perceived to be an existing problem. I guess they will ultimately be judged according to which side of the fence the judge is sitting on – or alternatively, by their results. *'Ye shall know them by their fruits'* (Luke: 6, 43) has always seemed to me a good criterion to use in evaluating any group or individual.

So let's get back to the Gülen Movement. First of all there is an official website[29]. You won't find the 'hidden agenda' of course, because that would, of necessity, be hidden. But you will find a very fascinating and comprehensive source of information about the man, his beliefs and goals. According to the brief bio, he *'is an authoritative mainstream Turkish Muslim scholar, thinker, author, poet, opinion leader and educational activist who supports interfaith and intercultural dialogue, science, democracy and spirituality and opposes violence and turning religion into a political ideology. Fethullah Gülen promotes cooperation of civilizations toward a peaceful world, as opposed to a clash'.* On this website you will find poetry and articles about education, the rights of women, the link between virtue and happiness . . . and other interesting topics too numerous to mention. You will find that Gülen cites as a source of his inspiration the 13th century Sufi mystic Mevlana Jalal al-Din Rumi, renowned for his inclusive philosophy of love and peace.

Wikipedia will tell you, not surprisingly, that the *Gülen Movement* is inspired by the teachings of Fethullah Hodja. A key concept is the Turkish word *Hizmet*, meaning *service*, which connotes using your talents for the common good without looking for personal reward. On the other hand, Gülen does

---

29 http://www.fethullahgulen.org/

not discourage followers from making money through business – merely encourages them to use some of their energies to help the less fortunate.

A recent *Time* magazine article[30] wrote about a meeting with members of the Gülen Movement in the eastern Turkish city of Diyarbakır. In an economically disadvantaged region of the country with a large Kurdish population, local businessmen have been raising money for the foundation of elementary schools and public reading rooms. While the article does say that *'many Turks view the Gulen Movement with suspicion'*, on the face of it, you'd have to think that the fruits of its efforts seem quite positive, even laudable.

According to another website called *'Gülen Inspired Schools'*[31], there are over a thousand such schools around the world, including 130 in the United States. Independent audits suggest that these schools produce excellent academic results, ranking them among the most successful in their respective countries. Interestingly, administrators deny any control by the Hodja, or a central body associated with him, unlike, say, Catholic Church-run schools. Investigators have found no evidence of religious teaching, Islamic or otherwise. On the contrary, Gülen has been quoted as saying, *"Studying physics, mathematics, and chemistry is worshipping God,"* and the common thread running through the schools seems to be a curriculum focusing on these modern subjects.

Sounds ok, on the whole, what do you think? Still, I have to confess I found one or two negatives in my searchings. An article in the *New York Times*[32] in 2006 reported that some of those Texas schools had been allegedly giving construction contracts and making other favourable deals with firms 'connected to' the Gülen movement. More seriously, Mr Gülen himself was apparently put on trial in 1999 for *'attempting to overthrow the government.'* Still, when you consider that the present Prime Minister of

---

30 http://www.time.com/time/world/article/0,8599,2115391,00.html?xid=newsletter-europe-weekly

31 http://gulenschools.org/

32 http://www.nytimes.com/2012/06/06/us/audits-for-3-georgia-charter-schools-tied-to-gulen-movement.html?_r=1

Turkey served prison time in those days for a similar offence, you'd have to think that the legal criteria must have been somewhat more stringent than we would expect in the US or New Zealand. In his younger days, the Hodja also apparently fell foul of the military authorities after the 1971 coup in Turkey, being arrested, tried and convicted. Not surprising, then, that he chooses to reside in the USA – although Turkish courts did clear him of all wrongdoing in 2008.

Anyway, ladies and gentlemen, I thank you for your patience in reading so far. I'm not here to be an apologist for Fethullah Gülen or any political or religious ideology. I merely want to outline the philosophies and fruits of two movements, and ask you to consider who you would prefer to see ruling the world.

On the one hand, let me present bottom-line accounting, out-of-control free-market capitalism, as championed by Wall Street bankers, multi-national corporations and the so-called mainstream media. Key elements of this ideology are: privatisation of state-owned enterprises, belt-tightening (especially for the middle and lower socio-economic classes), welfare cutbacks, labour-market flexibility and outsourcing of manufacturing to countries with lower wage costs. MBA management courses churn out white-colour clones who can manage any enterprise, without needing to know anything about the activity of the industry they are managing. Governments are hijacked by corporate and financial interests with no personal morality or patriotism whatsoever, whose only belief is in the power of money to buy whatever they want, and a philosophy, if you can call it that, based on a firm sense of personal entitlement to rape the planet of its resources and exploit its people wherever they may be. Reduced taxes for the wealthy are an important tool in economic management. Why should the taxpayer pay for schools, hospitals, post offices, railways, electricity supply, and relief for the unemployed and disadvantaged? The taxpayer's money is needed to bail out the banks when they have finished milking ma and pa small investors, superannuation funds and poor borrowers – and there's no one else in the capitalist system to defraud.

On the other hand, let's postulate a group of people with a personal morality based on religious beliefs, and a philosophy founded on a concept of altruistic service to the community. A group of people who operate without the need for a centralised bureaucratic structure, their operations inspired by a teacher with a vision of a better world and directed by their own confidence in the truth of his message. A group of people who, in spite of their lofty ideals, do not divorce themselves from the real world, but rather work within it, using their knowledge, skills and resources to provide educational opportunities and support to young people in their communities.

In the end, I guess, life choices are never so simple. I don't imagine you will get the opportunity to cast a vote directly for one or the other. But I like the sound of this[33]:

Along the winding road to The Truth A hero, all selfishness banished, The key to the mystery of creation in his heart, Weaves his way through time to reach his goal.

Moving ever upwards he breathes the air of eternity; He has met with Khidr: he knows the way. And to fellow wayfarers he gives the good news of dawn; A message of hope in a night of choking darkness.

In his hands burns a torch; he spreads light everywhere And he brightens the Way for all who would follow; His ascent radiates peace and serenity; His amber fragrance permeates every atom of creation.

Wherever he treads finds life and becomes green: The hills and valleys, plains and mountains are all dressed in color: And on every breeze is borne the perfume of spring; Blossoms appear, flowers burst into life, trees are quickened.

His mind nurtured ever by eternity, And everlasting melody flows from his lips: All he sees is the richly colored tapestry of life to come, The belief in which is part of his every being.

---

33 http://en.fgulen.com/broken-plectrum/2149-man-with-a-cause

14

True Religion in Turkey and Elsewhere

11 July 2012

We live in a godless world, and that's a fact. Now whether it's because God is actually dead, as Friedrich Nietsche asserted, or because He has just given up on the human race and planet Earth, and taken His attentions elsewhere, I can't say, but it must be one or the other. How did I come to this conclusion? I did what people usually do in this post-modern world when faced with a difficult question or an existential dilemma . . . I did a *Google* search. I keyed in *'true religion'*, and I want to share my findings with you. I must admit, I didn't check out all 226,000,000 results, but of the thirty-three on the first three pages, twenty-six were links to a brand of jeans. Sure, seven of them would take you to sites with a more spiritual content, but four of those were on page three – and I'm not sure how many Google-searchers get even that far.

Well, Nietzsche published his famous statement in 1882, so I can't claim to have made an astonishing new discovery. Nevertheless, as with all complex ideas, one can read and intellectually engage with it, but not immediately experience or internalise its full import. Many years ago, as a student in a senior English literature class, I remember our professor asking how many of us had read the Bible. Few hands were raised, and certainly not mine. *'Then how,'* asked the professor, *'can you presume to study English literature when you haven't read its single most important influence for most of the centuries of its development?'*

Later, as a teacher of literature myself, I would sometimes need to explain to my students a reference in a text we were studying. It shocked me a little to find how few students in a New Zealand high school had even second-hand knowledge of the best-known biblical stories. Interestingly, those who did were more likely to be of Maori or Polynesian, than European descent. The quotation is variously attributed to Jomo Kenyatta and Bishop Desmond Tutu, but it applies equally to New Zealand: *'When the white-men came, we* (Maori, African, Native American . .) *had the land and they had the Bible. They taught us to pray with our eyes closed, and when we opened them, we had the Bible and they had the land.'*

I have written elsewhere of how coming to Turkey gave me new insights into the influence of politics and government on the development of the 'belief' systems of Christianity. At the same time, I found myself looking with new eyes on the Muslim religion that was now all around me. Like Western visitors before me, I was fascinated by the call to prayer, emanating eerily from the minaret of my local mosque. As a child of the 60s, I turned to Yusuf Islam, aka Cat Stevens, for information. Not every Turk can tell you what the holy gentleman is saying, so, for those needing assistance, this is it:

Allāhu Akbar	*God is [the] greatest.*
Ash-hadu an-la ilaha illa llah	*I bear witness that there is no deity except God.*
Ash-hadu anna Muḥammadan-Rasulullah	*I bear witness that Muhammad is the Messenger of God.*
Hayya 'ala s-salah	*Come to prayer*
Hayya 'ala 'l-falah	*Come to success.*
Allāhu akbar	*God is great*
La ilaha illa-Allah	*There is no deity except God*

It's Arabic, of course, which bears a similar relationship to Turkish as does Latin to English – that is, it is the traditional language of religion and higher learning. To correct a misunderstanding in the minds of many Westerners, the word *Allah* is the Arabic for *God*, preceded by the definite article *al-*, and not the name of some pagan deity entirely unrelated to the focus of Christian worship. In the Muslim religion, Christians (and Jews) are *'People of the Book'*, part of the same great monotheistic tradition, and therefore brothers (and sisters) or at least cousins in religion.

Now no doubt some of you are thinking – this guy has been in Turkey so long, and seems so sympathetic, he's probably become a Muslim himself. But no. In the first place, I incline to the Mahatma Gandhi, Donovan school of thought. I'm equally Buddhist, Baptist, Jew and Muslim, and equally none of them. And in the second place, I have an aversion to pain, and a strong attachment to that intimate part of my anatomy the removal of which seems to be regarded by institutional Islam as an important component of true belief. This, then, brings me back to the problem I experienced above with my search for true religion.

Check all the sources you like, you'll find that religion is a difficult concept to tie down. The 19th century German philologist Max Müller wrote that the original meaning of the Latin word *religio,* from which our word religion is derived, was *'reverence for God or the gods, careful pondering of divine things'*. In other words, it was a personal business, a feeble attempt by human beings to deal with the metaphysical, existential problems that most of us encounter in the course of a lifetime. This denotation of religion you will still find in modern dictionaries. However, it is the conflict between this and the other meaning of the word that causes most of our difficulties. The other meaning of course, is an *'institutionalized system of religious attitudes, beliefs, and practices'*. It was institutional religion that persecuted Christians in Roman times, and which, when its turn came, used the tools of the Inquisition to torture and murder. It was institutional religion which Karl Marx called *'the opium of the people'* for its power to induce acceptance of oppression instead of revolt.

Well, the struggle goes on, not only between religions, but within them as well. I have no intention of examining the struggle between Christendom and Islam. Enough nonsense has been written elsewhere, based seemingly on the assumptions that such a thing as Christendom still exists, and that Islam has some kind of unified integrity. Similarly, the tension within Christianity between the individual search for spiritual truth and the need of the institution to control by the imposition of doctrinal and ritual uniformity are well documented. What I want to look at is the situation in contemporary Turkey where the forces of secular modernity are supposedly in conflict with the AK Party government, whose secret agenda is said to aim at returning the country to the Sharia rule of orthodox Islam.

The personification of secular modernity in Turkey is the founder of the Republic, Mustafa Kemal Atatürk, who inspired and united nationalist forces, building a nation from the ashes of the moribund Ottoman Empire. One of the six principles on which he established the new state was the separation of church (mosque) and government. He saw religion as an anchor holding back his people from taking their place among the world's modern states. To break the stranglehold of religion, he banned traditional forms of clothing (such as the fez), replaced the Arabic alphabet with a customised Latin-based one, outlawed the mystical dervish sects which constituted a serious threat to his programme of reform, and mandated the use of the Turkish language in place of Arabic in religious services – including the call to prayer. For eighteen years from 1932, the words heard from minarets in Turkey were these:

Tanrı uludur, Şüphesiz bilirim, bildiririm Tanrı'dan başka yoktur tapacak. Şüphesiz bilirim, bildiririm; Tanrı'nın elçisidir Muhammed. Haydin namaza, haydin felaha, Namaz uykudan hayırlıdır.

Well, there's something about the vernacular that appeals to populist philosophies, yet is anathema to organised religion. One could probably trace a correlation between the availability of the Christian Bible in English and other native tongues, and the long slow decline in religious observance in those countries. Probably Atatürk knew this. Surprisingly, then, it was the Democratic Party government of Turkey's first popularly elected Prime Minister, Adnan Menderes, that reinstituted the use of Arabic in Turkish mosques, among other Islam-friendly moves. Menderes epitomises for me some of the contradictions that perplex the foreigner in Turkey. He oversaw a period of rapid economic growth and Westernisation, while making major concessions to his majority Muslim electorate. He achieved a kind of superman reputation in his lifetime as a consequence of surviving a plane crash that killed most of his fellow passengers, yet ended his life on the gallows, hanged by the perpetrators of a military coup that seized power in Turkey in 1960.

Menderes was later exonerated, and his reputation restored to the extent that his name is honoured today in boulevards, airports and prestigious state high schools throughout the land. But the fact remains that he undoubtedly began the process of undoing Atatürk's secularising reforms that has continued under subsequent regimes. Many of those secular Turks mentioned above, who maintain that the AK Party government has a secret Islamic agenda, see signs of this in PM Erdoğan's moves to pull the teeth of the Turkish military. In Turkey, the army has been seen by 'secularists' as having an almost sacred role to ensure the sanctity of the secular state, to the extent that they have applauded the generals when they have staged coups to overturn democratically elected governments.

Somewhat ironically, then, the last such military regime, which seized power in 1981, was also happy to make major concessions to the Muslim electorate, appealing to religion and extreme nationalism in order to suppress left-wing dissent. When the generals stepped back and handed power over to a civil administration, their choice for Prime Minister was Turgut Özal, formerly MP for an overtly Islamic party. Again, somewhat ironically, the Prime Mister deposed by the coups of 1970 and 1981 was a certain Suleiman Demirel, who later returned to office and installed a puppet PM in his place, before having himself appointed President of the Republic. In spite of this, when I first came to Turkey in the mid-1990s, Demirel too seemed to have restored his reputation and become a pillar of Kemalist secularism.

In another strange mating of secularism and religiosity, Demirel's female successor Tansu Çiller, at the time a great symbol of Turkish progressiveness, formed a coalition with the Islamist Party of the day, allowing Necmettin Erbakan to become the republic's first openly Islamic Prime Minister. Erbakan's tenure was short-lived, however, and he was politely urged to stand down by the generals, in what has become known as Turkey's 'post-modern' coup of 1997.

Returning then to our consideration of religion above, it's hard to see much *'reverence for God or the gods, or careful pondering of divine things'* in all these political machinations. There is ample evidence in Turkey's recent history that secular politicians and even the military guardians of secular Kemalism have been only too ready to play the religion card when it suited their purposes. So it does seem a little hypocritical now for the same people, and/or their followers to ride the high horse and attack PM Erdoğan and his government for introducing relatively innocuous reforms such as allowing women wearing headscarves to study at university.

I do feel that a country such as Turkey, which struggles with serious inequalities of wealth distribution, could leave the building of mosques and the payment of religious leaders to local congregations and independent organisations. But funding of these by the state is not an innovation of the present government, and even the secular opposition are not interested in making such change an election issue. At the same time I have some sympathy for those who wish to see minarets continue as a feature of the modern Turkish skyline. I remember another of my professors drawing attention to an engraving of 17th century London, in which church spires were the prominent architectural feature. His point, as I recall, was that a comparison with the same view today might suggest something about modern-day priorities.

Of course, the problem is vastly more complicated, and I have no wish to oversimplify. Those 17th century London churches were representative of a religious establishment inextricably bound up with the government and the ruling elite of the day, and not necessarily a sign that their builders had any great interest in a search for spiritual truth. And I have similar misgivings when the muezzin of our local mosque wakes me around 5.30 these summer mornings with six minutes and 30 seconds of Arabic amplified by modern electronics and broadcast through loudspeakers attached to the highest point of his minaret. Perhaps he is genuine as he intones that extra line inserted into the morning edhan: *'As-salatu khayrun min an-nawm' (praying is better than sleeping)* – but I would credit him with more sincerity if I knew he had actually climbed the spiral staircase to the lofty balcony, and used the unassisted decibels that God had given him.

Well, I don't know if I have helped any of you here in your search for true religion. If the search comes to nothing, we can at least take consolation from the fact that globalisation is bringing our disparate institutional religions closer together. Witness the Shard Tower, recently opened in London, and now the highest building in Europe, financed, apparently by the Royal family of Qatar. And if you want a quick personal solution, get yourself a pair of those jeans.

15

The Last Word on Armenianism -
In search of solutions

13 August 2012

If you happened to be in Berlin recently, you may have indulged your musical appetite with an evening out at the *Young Euro Classic Music Festival*, a two-and-a-half week event taking place at the Konzerthaus on Gendarmenmarkt Square. The programme included orchestras from all over the world, African jazz, ballet, dance and choral groups, with the common factor of young people playing and enjoying music.

One of the concerts featured an assembly of musicians calling themselves the *Turkish-Armenian Youth Orchestra*, playing works by Beethoven, as well as by one Turkish and one Armenian composer. According to the festival website:

'For the first time, Young Euro Classic presents an Armenian-Turkish Youth Symphony Orchestra. Initiated by Young Euro Classic, this ensemble unites young musicians from Armenia and Turkey in one joint orchestra. This ambitious project has great symbolic importance, given the political tensions between the neighbouring countries of Turkey and Armenia. The young Turkish and

Armenian musicians distinguish themselves through the joy they take in their excellent music-making.'

The event attracted my attention because I had recently read an article in the *New York Times*[34] by a gentleman called Taner Akçam. In fact, because of its tone and content, the article received some small attention in our local Turkish newspaper as well. The title was *'Turkey's Human Rights Hypocrisy'*, and the writer, a well-known activist in the area of Armenian-Turkish relations, was drawing a connection between the contemporary situation in Syria, and the mass deaths of Armenians in the Ottoman Empire in 1915. The essence of Mr Akçam's argument was that Turks should shut up about what Bashar al-Assad is doing to his people in neighbouring Syria until the Turkish Government admits to carrying out genocide against the Armenian race, and (unstated but we may assume) pays appropriate reparations. According to him, Christians and other minorities in Syria are choosing to support al-Assad's murderous regime because of some strange connection in their minds between political freedom and Ottoman killings of Armenians in the 1st World War. Well, Mr Akçam can set his friends minds at rest, I think. Even if Turkey had the aim of wiping out *'Christians and other minorities'* (which I am pretty sure they don't) – it seems clear that they have no interest in invading and annexing Syria.

I'm not going to expend energy going through Akçam's article point by point to debate his weasel words and dubious logic, but I did pick up on one term that was new to me – *denialist*. It's not a word you'll find in older dictionaries, but it's a pretty useful one, I'm sure you'll agree. It goes beyond the Freudian term *denial*, perhaps because that word was losing its force from over-use. When you call someone a *denialist*, the *–ist* ending adds extra power to the criticism since it implies some kind of political/ideological conspiracy. The beauty of it is, as was the case with the earlier word in popular usage, it does away with the need for further debate, since you have at one blow established, without need for actual proof, that your opponent's arguments are

---

34 http://www.nytimes.com/2012/07/20/opinion/turkeys-human-rights-hypocrisy.html

flying in the face of all scientific and historical evidence. So Turks are engaging in *denialism* on the issue of Armenian genocide – end of argument.

I guess that's roughly where I started from when I first arrived in Turkey. Not that I knew a lot about it, but I knew what pretty much everyone knows: Turks slaughtered Armenians, right? In 1915, right? One-and-a-half million of them, right? That's where Hitler got his inspiration for the Jewish Holocaust, right? Then I started to read about the Ottoman Empire that ruled what is now Turkey and much else in the region for over six hundred years until it whimpered out of existence in 1923. I learnt that Armenians were a respected *millet* within the Ottoman Empire along with Jews and Orthodox Christians; granted freedom to worship, use their own language, bury their dead in their own cemeteries, educate their children in their own schools, run businesses, get rich, rise to high positions in society . . . and my curiosity was aroused. Why would the Ottoman government suddenly decide to genocide these people?

Our local newspaper is running a series of articles during the month of Ramazan about significant mosques around the country. One article featured the Aksaray Mosque of Pertevniyal Valide Sultan, mother of the 19th century Ottoman Padishah, Abdulaziz. The writer credits the building to the architect Sarkis Balyan, five generations of whose family served as builders and architects to the Ottoman regime through the eighteenth and nineteenth centuries. I checked him out on a website called *World Architecture Map*[35] and I learned that he lived from 1835-1899, but the space for *Place of Birth* was blank, and alongside *Nationality* there were three question marks (???).

Still, pretty much everyone knows that people with surnames ending in –yan or –ian are more than likely of Armenian ethnicity, and *Wikipedia* confirms that about the Balyans. So, credit where credit's due – five generations of this Armenian family worked for the Ottoman dynasty and were responsible for the building of some of the city's best known landmarks: the imperial palaces of Çırağan (now a five-star Kempinski hotel) and

---

35 http://www.worldarchitecturemap.org/architects/sarkis-balyan

Dolmabahçe, along with numerous mosques, public buildings and major factories. I haven't been able to confirm the facts, but I would make an educated guess that, despite his Armenian ethnicity, Sarkis Balyan was an Ottoman citizen, born in Istanbul. I can't say for sure why the WAM people couldn't establish that one way or the other, but I have my suspicions.

Still, I hear you. Just because there were a few successful and respected Armenians in the empire it doesn't mean genocide didn't happen. Being a pillar of society didn't save many Jews in Nazi Germany, did it? Nevertheless, you take my point. I wanted to know why the Ottoman state, after five centuries of relatively peaceful coexistence, would suddenly decide that genocide of Armenians was the way to go. Of course, once I started, I found that I had opened a can of worms. One question led to another, and another, and another, and I can truthfully tell you that I cannot give you a conclusive answer on this one. What I can say, however, is that labelling Turks 'denialist' in no way does justice to the complexity of the issue. Undoubtedly a horrifying number of Armenian people lost their lives in a tragic series of events in 1915, set in train by officers of the Ottoman Empire. This much seems to be accepted by all, but thereafter, important questions arise:

- Were these events part of a state-sponsored programme whose aim was the extermination of a race? Proponents of the case for genocide claim to have seen official documents proving this. Opponents claim that at least some of these documents are falsified.

- How many died? Obviously, in the circumstances, it is impossible to get an accurate count, but numbers vary enormously depending on which case is being argued. Still, even the lowest estimates seem to accept that several hundred thousand died – clearly an unacceptable number.

- Is Turkey responsible? Whatever happened, happened in the last years of the Ottoman Empire, which was not a nationalist state.

Europeans had for centuries chosen to label the Ottoman rulers *Turks*, and their empire *Turkey*, but this is a distortion of the facts, a bit like outsiders calling citizens of the USA *Yanks*. Turks, incidentally, tend to refer to the United Kingdom as *İngiltere*, and its citizens as *İngliz*. The Ottoman Empire was defeated, along with its ally Germany, in the First World War, and thereafter divided among the conquerors, principally Britain, France, Italy and Greece. The modern Republic of Turkey was established in 1923 after a struggle by nationalist freedom-fighters who expelled invading forces from Anatolia and Istanbul, marginalising and subsequently abolishing the Ottoman Sultanate and its government. So there is only a tenuous connection between the perpetrators of whatever happened in 1915, and the present-day Turkish Republic.

- Is what happened to the Armenians comparable to Nazi German measures to exterminate Jews? First of all, the Germans set up a bureaucratic machine and invested in plant and facilities to expedite their scheme. There was large-scale state propaganda designed to justify Nazi actions. The Germans invaded other sovereign states and carried out their policy in those places also (France, Poland and Greece, for example). As far as I am aware, none of these factors was present in the case of Ottoman Armenians. It is also clear that extermination was the primary object of the Nazi German programme. The Ottoman aim was to remove/relocate people perceived as a serious security threat at a time when their state was at war and fighting for its survival on at least three fronts. Third, there is a long history in Europe (not only in Germany) of state-sponsored discrimination and violence towards Jews. This was definitely not the case in the Ottoman Empire (see above). Finally, there was no context in which Nazi German actions could be justified. The Jewish people posed no security threat to Germany and gave no provocation. On the other hand, Armenian nationalist groups had been carrying out terrorist activities in Ottoman territory for decades. As American military personnel in Iraq testify, in a guerrilla warfare situation, it is by no means easy to distinguish dangerous militants from law-abiding villagers – and remember, the Ottomans were operating on their own soil, with at least some modicum of moral authority. Further, it is also historically verifiable (as I have written elsewhere) that Russian Imperial expansion into Ottoman territory had involved the incitement of Christian minorities (including Armenians) to revolt against their lawful government, followed by large-scale killing, terrorising and displacement of Muslims from the areas they conquered.

OK, I admit I am working from secondary sources here. Like most of you, I don't have the time or the language skills to check primary documents. I am not employed and paid a salary by any university's Department of Genocide Studies. I can say, however, that I have read a broad sample of the literature on both sides of this question, and I can assure you that there are some quite reputable scholars who question the application of the term 'genocide' to this Armenian business. One in particular you may like to check out is Justin McCarthy, Professor of History at the University of Louisville, Kentucky. One of his publications is actually available as a free eBook[36], so take a look.

Now, I know that, if you are a follower of Armenian Genocide Studies, you will be aware that McCarthy and others who attempt to balance the ledger on this issue, come in for a deal of criticism, and not simply on a scholarly level. I read an article[37] recently by a lady identifying herself as a *Latin Americanist* (there's that *-ist* again). She was waxing warm on the Armenian issue, and informed the reader that our Taner Akçam (above) had received death threats for his outspokenness. She went on to say that

---

36 http://www.globaled.org/WhoAreTheTurksebook.pdf

37 http://www.huffingtonpost.com/mikaela-luttrellrowland/armenian-genocide-commemoration-day_b_1447786.html?ref=impact

he 'fears prosecution' if he ever sets foot in his native Turkey. Interestingly, then, the *Wikipedia* entry reveals that this 'wanted man' attended the politically-charged funeral of Hrant Dink in Istanbul in 2007, and managed to get safely back to his job of criticising Turks and their country at Clark University, Massachusetts. I'm not saying that the poor fellow hasn't received a death threat or two. I even got one myself while teaching at a prestigious high school in Auckland, New Zealand. The house of UCLA Professor Stanford Shaw was bombed in 1977 after he published a book on Turkish history in which he questioned the accuracy of Armenian genocide arguments, and Armenian ultra-nationalist organizations (to borrow a phrase) were responsible for the deaths of forty-two Turkish diplomatic staff abroad between 1973 and 1994, so make what you will of that.

As for the personal attacks on '*denialist*' scholars, that *Wikipedia* entry on Taner Akçam names a certain Vahakn Dadrian as his academic mentor. I checked him out and learned that Dadrian is a '*towering figure in the field of Armenian genocide history*'. The quote is attributed to an academic by the name of David Bruce MacDonald. He too has a very nice entry in *Wikipedia*, but the managers of the site warn that '*a major contributor to this article appears to have a close relationship with its subject*'. Getting back to Mr Dadrian, I further learned that he had been dismissed from his position as Professor of Sociology at the State University College in Geneseo, New York for sexually molesting an eighteen year-old student. According to the report[38] I read, Mr Dadrian had escaped punishment for a similar offense ten years earlier by pleading 'cultural differences'. Given that the learned professor had pursued his academic studies at reputable universities in Europe and the USA, you'd think he might have gleaned some understanding of acceptable teacher-student behaviour in Western cultures. Anyway, the excuse apparently didn't wash the second time he was caught.

The *Wikipedia* entry on Akçam states that he is '*recognised as a leading international authority on the subject*' (their quotes) of Armenian genocide. If you check the referenced footnote, you'll find that the words are

---

38 http://albarchive.merlinone.net/mweb/wmsql.wm.request?oneimage&imageid=5599449

attributed to a David Holthouse of the *Southern Poverty Law Centre*. If you follow that lead, you'll learn that the SPLC published an apology for that particular article and retracted claims made therein that, among other untruths, another scholar arguing for a more balanced view of the issue, Guenter Lewy, was in the pay of the Turkish Government. But I'm not here to blacken anyone's name - merely to suggest that there may be more to this business than simply 'truth' and '*denialism*'.

I am not at all a reader of horror literature, but I am about to finish a book that is seriously frightening me. Probably the scariest thing about it is, it is not a work of fiction. The writer is Kevin Phillips, a political and economic commentator from Lichfield, Connecticut, and former strategist for the US Republican Party. In the book '*American Theocracy*'[39], he posits an unholy alliance conjoining big oil, the finance industry and fundamentalist Christianity which he claims has taken over the GOP and pretty much the governing of the United States. To put the thesis of a 400-page book in a nutshell, the 'FIRE' sector (finance, insurance, real estate) is enriching a small elite by encouraging indebtedness at every level of society (spend like there's no tomorrow – it's your patriotic duty!); as US oil runs out, it becomes necessary to control the major global areas of supply (did you ever believe Iraq was not about oil?); and fundamentalist Christian leaders hold that an inerrant Bible justifies man's exploitation of the environment, salvation is by faith alone (which means no need for social welfare programmes, hence no taxes), unbelievers must be converted or destroyed, and the end-times are coming when true believers will be 'raptured' and the last battles will be played out in the Middle East, home of the anti-Christ and his evil followers (Muslims).

All this wouldn't be particularly relevant here, except that, in my rummaging around on the Internet, I learned that Taner Akçam had been giving talks to an organisation called CSI – aka the *Christian Solidarity Foundation*[40]. On their web page, their CEO has this to say:

---

39 http://www.amazon.com/American-Theocracy-Politics-Religion-Borrowed/dp/067003486X

40 http://www.csi-usa.org/

'CSI is unique. It is currently the only organization working in the field to free slaves captured by Islamic jihadists [another -ist] *during Sudan's civil war, and we are one of the few organizations to shine a light on the disappearance, forced conversions and forced marriages of Christian women in Egypt. My colleagues have repeatedly traveled to terror-torn Iraq to stand in solidarity with that country's beleaguered Christian community, and CSI supports the tiny remnant of Christians who remain in Turkey following the great anti-Christian Genocide and its devastating after-effects.*

'These are troubled times for Christians and other religious minorities in the broader Islamic Middle East where an upsurge of radical Islamic supremacism [that –ism again] *threatens their very existence. The situation is especially dire in Syria, Egypt, Iraq and Iran.'*

Well, hate comes easy to human nature, I guess. Unfortunately, there are many organisations hiding behind words like *peace, freedom, truth* and *democracy* while pursuing programmes of discrimination, prejudice and violence. There is a wonderful novel, *'Birds Without Wings'*, by the English novelist Louis de Bernieres. It deals with events surrounding the time of that *'great anti-Christian Genocide'* in a rather more even-handed manner. A minor character, Daskalos Leonidas, is schoolteacher in the small Anatolian village of Eskibahçe where most of the story takes place. The village is a microcosm of the Ottoman Empire, with Muslims, Greek and Armenian Christians getting along as they had for centuries, before the great upheavals of the 20th century tore them apart. The teacher is a lonely bitter man who sees his mission as being to educate his Greek Christian neighbours in 'their own culture' and to foster a spirit of nationhood which they will then fight to achieve. The result is the disaster of the Greek-Turkish War and the tragedy of the population exchanges that followed. I wish the organisers of that Berlin Festival well, and hope that their attempts to demonstrate the power of music to heal wounds and unite souls will not be in vain.

Excavated 9th century Byzantine monastery
of St Satyros, Küçükyalı, Istanbul

The author in front of Piyale Pasha Mosque, Kasımpaşa, Istanbul

A selection of Turkish wines –
the industry is making a comeback
after a tough millennium or so

Albania/Shqiperie – maligned
or ignored but well worth a visit

Works of Salman Rushdie,
translated into Turkish and
readily available from a
local bookstore

Replica Viking longboat in Ribe,
Denmark – not only took
them to America but
Constantinople too

Monuments to God and Mammon in the
new Turkey – Ataşehir, Istanbul

What's left of the wondrous Temple of Artemis in situ – Selçuk, Turkey

Jesus turns water into wine –
Ceiling mosaic, Kariye
Museum, Istanbul

Archeological excavations beside
the new Metro station,
Yenikapı, Istanbul

Beautiful carved capital found at Magnesia-on-the-Meander.
When unearthed, the heads were still on the bodies,
later removed by persons unknown

18th century mosque of Musa the Circassian,
Magnesia-on-the-Meander

Demonstrating for democracy – Taksim, Istanbul, June 2013

16

The Circumcision Debate - To snip or not to snip?

18 September 2012

An intriguing debate is raging in Germany after a district court in the Rhineland city of Cologne (Köln) ruled in May that a doctor who performed a circumcision operation on a four-year-old boy, had committed an assault, despite the fact that the mother had given her consent. The court went on to acquit the doctor on the grounds that the legal situation vis-a-vis circumcision is somewhat unclear. Nevertheless, a local event escalated into an international storm involving German Chancellor Angela Merkel, Israeli President Shimon Peres and other high-level political leaders, with implications reaching far beyond the narrow boundaries of the original case. Most Jews and Muslims see circumcision as an important cultural rite of passage for their male offspring. With respect to Jews, Germany has a fair swag of historical guilt to live down, without aggravating matters by seeming to renew discrimination. Muslims are a significant and growing minority in the population, with Turks forming the largest group (four to five percent).

Political leaders like Merkel have a difficult row to hoe in Western Europe these days with the rise of popular fears focusing on immigration from poorer countries, Islamic fundamentalism and terrorism, public perception that their own culture and traditions are under threat, coupled with deteriorating economic conditions in the European Union. Voter interest in extreme right-wing parties appears to be growing at the same time as minority groups are expressing frustration with what they perceive as local resentment and intolerance.

Prejudice undoubtedly exists, fuelled by the usual problems associated with an influx of immigrants from different cultural backgrounds. The situation is, of course, not clear-cut. Far right politicians are playing to a significant sector of public opinion. A majority of Germans apparently favour a ban on the practice of circumcision for religious purposes. Their government rarely permits dual citizenship for immigrants from outside the European Union. The Swiss have imposed a ban on the construction of minarets on mosques. At the same time, Muslims, Turks especially, are playing increasingly high-profile roles in their adopted homes – French, German and Swiss national football teams, for example, seem happy to welcome players with Islamic roots.

In addition, the circumcision issue is further complicated by questions relating to the rights of children. When two apparently inalienable human rights conflict, resolution is not easy to find. In this case, we have the right of a group to continue a religious or cultural practice, versus the right of a child to retain its God-given bodily integrity without suffering physical harm. Drafting a law which will satisfy proponents of both positions is the problem currently facing German legislators.

But of course, it's not just a German problem. On the microcosmic level, one of the most important decisions facing parents-to-be in many Western countries is what to do about the little chap's foreskin, should they happen to produce a boy-child. Surgical removal is not common in European countries, but widely carried out in the USA – though statistics show a decline since the 1970s. In Jewish and Islamic communities, there's not much to discuss. Societal pressure makes the decision, and the prepuce comes off.

How does it come off? Well, in Jewish circles, I gather, there is a trained person (*mohel*) who stretches the foreskin of the eight-day-old baby and quickly slices off as much as he can without damaging the rest of the little fellow's procreative equipment. Islamic tradition prefers waiting until the boy is older – somewhere between seven and ten years of age, and the method is similar. These days, there is a tendency towards hospital circumcision at birth, or performing the operation in a clinic with anaesthetic if done when the lad is older. In Western countries, the preference is for circumcising within a few days of birth, and involves a lengthier operation with more surgical tools. Generally, anaesthetic is used, but most sources I read suggest that parents should request this, because some doctors don't bother.

It's a quirky thing, isn't it? Obvious questions arise here, in particular: why would you cut off a normal part of a healthy baby's (or child's, or man's) anatomy? Especially in such a sensitive area of the body, crucial for the survival of the species. Where did the practice originate?

Well, it seems the origins of circumcision are lost in the mists of time, but most authorities agree that the earliest recorded foreskin removal ceremonies were conducted by the ancient Egyptians. Interestingly, the operation often seems to have been associated with some kind of religious ritual or initiation rite, and to have been fairly public. Egyptian paintings show grown men undergoing the procedure, and as far as can be surmised, the purpose was a test of manhood, demonstrating one's ability to endure pain. OK, that's one reason, then – and perhaps, in a primitive warrior society, there is a case to be made for such tests. However, there must be more to it than that, to have justified the continuation of circumcision down to the present day.

As far as Jews are concerned, the practice goes back to Father Abraham's covenant with God, way back when. God pretty much promised Abraham the Earth, but for his side of the bargain, Abraham had to have his foreskin removed – harsh treatment for a ninety-nine year-old guy! Anyway, you can find it all there (the story, not the foreskin), in the Old Testament Book of Genesis, Chapter 17, Verses 10-14: '*he that is eight days old shall be circumcised among you*', your own kids, relatives, servants, slaves, the lot;

'and the uncircumcised man child whose flesh of his foreskin is not circumcised, that soul shall be cut off from his people.'

The Islamic position is a little less clear, since there is, apparently, no instruction about it in the Quran. However, Muslims tend to accept most of the Old Testament teachings, and certainly regard Abraham as a Prophet of God, so by and large they go along with it. From a societal point of view such practices tend to forge a sense of belonging to a group, and also serve to distinguish members from non-members, so again, you can see the rationale. By extension, that probably explains a reason sometimes put forward by modern-day parents: all the other male members of the family had their male members trimmed, and we don't want the little fellow feeling that there's something wrong with him. Islamic scholars, however, seem to be of the opinion that conversion to the faith does not absolutely require surgical modification of the male sex organ.

Anyway, let's move on to consider other justifications offered in more recent times for the continued practice, especially in the absence of religious or long-standing cultural tradition. Towards the end of the 19th century, a time when sex had acquired something of a negative reputation, particularly in Britain and the United States, members of the medical profession were recommending circumcision as a cure for *'masturbatory insanity'*. Individuals so cured, it was said, would be healthier, live longer and be more energetic and productive. Interestingly, proponents of this argument also favoured female circumcision (clitoridectomy) for much the same reasons. As an example of this line of thinking, I have to share this quotation with you. The speaker is Dr John Harvey Kellogg (of Corn Flakes fame), who considered his commercial breakfast cereal effective in preventing masturbation. In addition:

"Covering the organs with a cage has been practiced with entire success. A remedy which is almost always successful in small boys is circumcision . . . The operation should be performed by a surgeon <u>without administering an anaesthetic</u>, as the brief pain attending the operation will have a salutary effect upon the mind, especially if it be connected with the idea of punishment, as it may

well be in some cases. The soreness which continues for several weeks interrupts the practice, and if it had not previously become too firmly fixed, it may be forgotten and not resumed."

I have an early memory of being bathed by my mother – I must have been around three years old – and I guess I was experimentally examining my little doodle. *'Don't touch it,'* warned my mum, and she told me the cautionary tale of a young lad in the neighbourhood who played with his appendage and it had to be cut off. The lesson was effective, at least for a while, and it was some years before I summoned the courage for further experimentation. In mum's favour, I have to thank her that she refrained from having me punitively circumcised – though perhaps my father must share the gratitude, since he had also retained his manhood intact.

Hygiene is often cited as a reason for male circumcision, and there is some evidence that infections can occur in uncircumcised males. There is also a condition known as *phimosis* (the inability to retract the foreskin over the head of the penis) which is sometimes treated by circumcision. Some doctors argue that urinary tract infections occur less in circumcised babies, and also that there is a reduced risk of penile cancer in later life. Perhaps the most powerful argument in favour of circumcision these days is the claim that removal of the foreskin reduces the risk of sexually transmitted diseases, especially HIV, at least in countries where the rate of infection is high – so for many proponents, no further justification is necessary.

If you are the prospective parent of a new boy child, clearly there is no shortage of arguments in favour of having the little man's foreskin removed. What about the other side of the debate? Undoubtedly there are many uncircumcised grown men in the world leading relatively normal, well-adjusted, productive lives, as yet untouched by AIDS or cancer of the penis. What of them? Are they just lucky, or is there a case to be made for leaving your male child whole and uncut? In my roamings on the internet, I came across the website of an organisation calling itself the *Circumcision Resource Center*, and I really recommend you to take a look. One of the first things I noticed on their home page was the claim that most of their directors are Jewish. Another item that caught my eye was a quotation on the banner by Michael de Montaigne: *"Nothing is so firmly believed as what we least know."*

Well, let me say loudly and clearly that I am not going to go criticising anyone's religion or strongly held cultural beliefs. Biblical scholars and historians of ancient Israel apparently harbour doubts about the historical validity of events and personages featuring in the Book of Genesis but if Abraham's covenant with God is important for you, then nothing much remains to be said. That will be the crucial factor in determining your parental responsibilities in this matter.

I don't know how much pain tolerance remains an unspoken but important element in some people's view of a child's passage to manhood. Call me a wimp, but I freely admit that I would not willingly submit to the removal of any part of my anatomy, let alone in that nether region, without a very convincing life-or-death medical argument, and certainly not without serious pain relief. However, in defence of my virility, I would like to offer the words of my childhood dentist, in the days when teeth were excavated by slowly spinning drills, sometimes even treadle-powered, without the benefit of local anaesthetic. Through mists of pain and watering eyes, I recall his gruff Scottish voice remarking, *"Well, laddie, those Germans widnae hae got much out o' you!"* I understood he was comparing his dental ministrations to Gestapo techniques of interrogation, well known to my post-war generation. Later, at the replica English grammar school I attended, I took my canings, as did most of my peers, without a fuss. More recently, a Turkish orthopaedic surgeon, realigning my dislocated elbow, observed that my pain tolerance was quite high, so I don't feel the need for more intimate proof.

The question of belonging is undoubtedly an important one, especially in all-male environments such as boarding schools, military barracks and prisons. Such communities can be unforgiving of anyone seen as different. I'm not so sure about the family argument though. Little boys may ask, *'Why is daddy's hair black and mine is orange?'* They may ask about different eye colour and so on. As a parent, you give the child an answer. Perhaps circumcising the kid might save the father's embarrassment, though, if he felt obliged to explain that *'Grandpa and grandma had mine cut off.'*

As for other claims for the benefits of circumcision, genital health and hygiene, most sources I checked agreed that the evidence is not powerfully persuasive. It seems that a little boy's foreskin rarely retracts in early childhood, and there is no cause for treatment unless it becomes a problem in teenage years. In modern societies, with readily available bathrooms, running hot water and soap, personal cleanliness is less of a difficulty than it may have been in waterless Middle Eastern deserts or medieval cities. The incidence of urinary tract infections is not high in babies, and when it occurs, may be attributable to other factors besides the existence of a foreskin. The same appears to be true for penile cancer in adults, and it is questionable whether the slight reduction in risk justifies the removal of a part of the body which the Creator, in His (or Her) infinite wisdom, saw fit to attach to His (or Her) highest creation. There is evidence that circumcision provides some reduced risk from sexually transmitted diseases, especially AIDS, but most of this evidence comes from poorer countries where the rate of infection is high, and again, seems to be a less convincing argument in more advanced societies. Also, other factors can be said to play an important role, in particular the practice (or not) of promiscuous unprotected sex.

Finally, there is the question, implied above, of why the male sex organ comes with a foreskin attached. First, there is the obvious function of protecting the sensitive head of the penis. One source I came across compared it to the eyelid's role in protecting the eye. Second, there is the medical fact that the foreskin contains nerves and blood vessels which make it also highly sensitive, increasing the pleasure of sexual contact. Admittedly, though, this may be a reason for Dr Kellogg's recommendations (see above). Finally, it has been suggested that the existence of the foreskin increases pleasure for the woman also in the sex act because it reduces friction and dryness. Of course, reducing such pleasure for the woman is, as far as I am aware, the major argument for female circumcision, or genital mutilation, as is the preferred term these days. Interestingly, use of the term is not extended to males, though the ancient Greeks apparently considered it so, finding the practice abhorrent.

Well, I will continue to follow the progress of German lawmakers in finding a solution acceptable to all sides in this debate. In the end, I suspect, in the interests of peace and social harmony, they will be obliged to leave the decision to snip or not to snip to the families concerned, while legislating to ensure that the procedure is carried out in authorised hospitals or clinics by qualified medical practitioners using some form of anaesthetic. That's probably as much as we can hope for in this less-than-perfect world.

17

Cultural difference - Turkish camels everywhere!

1 October 2012

It's the opening sequence of the 2004 Turkish Sci-Fi spoof *"G.O.R.A."* We're on the flight deck of an enormous inter-galactic spacecraft from the planet of the same name. The flight crew are speaking English. There's no emergency and no panic. It's a normal routine landing. *"Please ensure your seatbelt is fastened, your tray table is stowed away and your seat is in the upright position." "Commander, the system is f—king activated sir." "Pressure is f—king stable sir." "What are the f—king coordinates?"*

In a later sequence, on Planet Earth, Arif, the main character, gives a ride to an old villager. He wants to play music but the old guy objects. *"I don't like foreign music,"* he says. *"They could be swearing at my mother and I wouldn't know." "Don't worry,"* says Arif. *"This band is very young. They wouldn't know your mother."* He starts the track and the words erupt from the speaker – *"Motherf—ker yeah, motherf—ker yeah!"*

Now I don't want you to give the wrong impression here. Turks are quite capable of swearing, and their language is rich in words that you wouldn't use in front of your mother, father, or baby sister. But that's the point I want to make here. On the whole, there are still rules in Turkey, written and unwritten, governing when it is appropriate to use such words, and when not. Cem Yılmaz, the writer of the G.O.R.A. screenplay was poking fun at the apparent lack of such rules in the USA and other Western cultures.

I'm not a big follower of the latest trends in popular music. I haven't even glanced at *MTV* for years. Occasionally my students give me a glimpse into what's going on when they ask me what a certain word means in the lyrics of a song they've been listening to. My main link to Western pop culture comes from my visits to the gym, as my companions and I sweat to the rhythm of rap, hip-hop and electronic rock. I have to confess, the first time I heard the young lady from *20 Fingers* chanting, *"You gotta lick it, before we kick it"*, I was mildly shocked. Since then I have become less sensitive, and I scarcely blush when the guy from *2 Live Crew* lets me into the intimate details of The Way he Likes to . . . tie his shoe laces (Not!). Or Enrique Iglesias hammers out the alternative version of *"Tonight I'm Lovin' You"*.

On the other hand, on the occasional shopping expedition with my own good lady, when we find ourselves in some up-market trendy women's store, and the same lyrics are wafting over Istanbul matrons choosing fashion wear with their young daughters, a mischievous devil within urges me to offer a Turkish translation to the store manager.

This line of thought takes me nostalgically back to a more naïve time when my kids were teenagers, and I confiscated a *Red Hot Chilli Peppers* cassette on the grounds that, in my paternal opinion, the lyrics were not appropriate for the tender ears of my own 14 year-old daughter. I did reimburse her for the purchase price, however, and I can't be sure that she didn't immediately replace it, being more careful to use earphones around the house in future. Nevertheless, I felt I had done my fatherly duty. I'm just grateful I don't have to deal with a nymphet daughter these days getting advice from Benny Benassi and his lady friend on How to *get their Satisfaction*.

Turkish parents complain about their kids, but really they don't know how lucky they are. Check out these lyrics from the current Turkish Top 40:

I'm Tired[41], sings the girl. *I'm drifting away with the wind. I don't know if the end will be good or bad. I am so much in love I wish this feeling for all my friends. But sometimes, this love brings such pain, I can wish it on my enemies.*

and another one . . .

Don't Hold Back[42], says the guy. *Why do you keep your distance? You said, Close your eyes and I'll be there. You said, There is no obstacle to love. But what about touching and hugging? Don't hold back! If you miss me, if you can't live without me, don't hold back!*

Turkish teachers also complain about their students, but I find it hard to sympathise. The last time I taught in New Zealand, I had the experience of being eyeballed by a diminutive twelve year-old and called a "F—king W—ker". When I mentioned the incident to the school principal, the first thing he asked me was if there was anything I might have done to provoke the lad. I expect to retire from the profession before I have to listen to the Turkish equivalent from a student here.

Young, and not-so-young women from Western nations, however, sometimes find themselves on the receiving end of unwelcome attentions from young Turkish guys on the street. The reason is two-fold. In the first instance, Turkish girls are (or most of them anyway) very much under the protection of their families. It's not as easy for a Turkish guy to satisfy his sexual appetites out of wedlock as it is for his counterpart in the USA or New Zealand. Also, the impression these Turkish guys get of Western women from their portrayal in pop culture is one of sexual availability. This impression is reinforced by the undoubted fact that Turkey fulfils the role of sex tourist destination for middle-aged European women that Thailand plays for their menfolk. After one or two disturbing experiences, young Western visitors may be tempted to use an English obscenity (or learn its

41 http://www.sarki-sozleri.net/sila-yoruldum

42 http://sarki.alternatifim.com/data.asp?ID=180845&sarki=Kasma&sarkici=Yal%FDn

Turkish equivalent) to discourage unwanted attentions. As a general rule – Don't. A good Turkish girl is more likely to use a phrase equating to *"Shame on you"*. Anything stronger may only serve to aggravate the situation. The same goes for rejecting the determinedly importunate carpet-seller or hotel tout. Learning the Turkish for "I don't want one" (*Istemiyorum*) and uttering it in a firm tone will generally have the desired affect.

Something that struck me when I came to Turkey back in the late 90s was the absence of street graffiti. Sure, I know it's an artistic genre, and I fully appreciate the skill it takes to execute in its highest forms. However, not everyone can appreciate such works of art when they appear on the newly constructed pristine white wall around his house. For sure, I'm seeing more of such street art in Istanbul these days, and also the less artistic variety with obscenities, often in English. Still to be seen, though, are those touchingly amateurish outpourings of a young male heart: *"Ayshe I love you – Forgive me!"*

I am sure others like me will have had the following experience or something similar. Heading out on my bicycle one Sunday morning with the intention of stopping by the seaside for breakfast, I paused to buy two simits from a street vendor. As it happened, I had only a twenty-lira note, which the guy couldn't change. He insisted, however, that I take the simits and I could pay him at some future time. In fact I paid him on my return, having changed the note elsewhere. Far from being impressed with my scrupulous honesty, the chap seemed almost disappointed. His giving me the simits had been a good deed that God would undoubtedly reward – and my repaying him to some extent detracted from its merit.

Now I know that I am sometimes accused of lauding Turkey to the skies, and overlooking its faults. In part this is deliberate, in the sense that I am aware of the bad press that this country commonly suffers from, and these essays are an attempt to balance the ledger. Nevertheless, there are certainly cultural peculiarities that visitors to Turkey would be well advised to beware of. In April 2000 several planeloads of English football fans arrived in Istanbul to support Leeds United in its UEFA Cup match against the local team Galatarsaray. Accounts vary as to exactly what happened. Bar owners in the Taksim entertainment area said that a glass had been broken in a Turkish youth's face and that drunken approaches had been made to local women. Some said that revellers had mixed the powerful local spirit rakı with beer instead of the usual water. It was also suggested that the Turkish flag had been treated in a disrespectful way.

Whatever the reasons, fights broke out in nearby streets, and two Leeds fans died from knife wounds. English supporters, and the media back home were genuinely shocked. In the minds of some, the deaths amounted to murder, and feelings persist that the Turkish justice system failed to view the events of that night with the seriousness they warranted. They may well be right, but there are lessons to be studied by visitors to Turkey from foreign lands.

- First, public drinking and drunkenness are not very common, and generally frowned upon. Turks are quite capable of going out with friends to a restaurant of an evening without drinking alcohol at all. Don't assume your hometown attitudes to drinking and a fun night out are the same everywhere.

- Most Turks are very patriotic, and they strongly identify with their flag as a symbol of national pride. If you're not looking for big trouble, don't disrespect it.

- Some Turkish men do actually carry offensive/defensive weapons, and it is as well to be aware of this possibility before getting into a fight. At the time of the Leeds incident one of the English fans was quoted as saying, *"We didn't know they was tooled up."* Do your homework before getting on the plane.

- Fighting is a very serious business for most Turkish men, and inextricably tied up with the masculine sense of honour. Once a fight starts, it may not end until someone is dead, or seriously injured. Consequently, bystanders in Turkey will rarely allow an argument between two guys to come to blows. Strangers will intervene, for example, to keep road-ragers apart. For the same reason, it is incumbent upon the antagonists so separated not to be seen to be too easily discouraged from pursuing the fray. It may take two or three peacemakers to hold each honour-bound combatant until calm is restored. In general, it's better to avoid getting into a fight if you possibly can.

A more recent cinematic work from the Turkish comedian Cem Yılmaz, is the 2010 film, *Ottoman Cowboys* (*Yahşi Batı* in Turkish). Aziz and Lemi are two Ottoman officials charged by their Sultan with a mission to the President of the United States. The year is 1881, and our two Eastern gentlemen are sharing a stagecoach with an English couple, an elderly chap of aristocratic demeanour, and his younger wife.

"Are you French?" asks the lady. *"Oh no, madame,"* answers Lemi Bey. *"I'm Ottoman." "You ride camels don't you?"* inquires the Englishman with heavy sarcasm. *"Camels?"* replies Aziz Bey. *"Yes, every time. Always. Camels every-where."* Then in an aside to his companion, in Turkish, *"They always say that. It's the only thing they know."*

In fact, if you see a camel on your visit to Turkey, chances are it's there to provide photo ops for tourists who might otherwise be disappointed. If you want to visit the country with the largest population of camels, better go to Australia.

18

Albanian Independence Day

1 December 2012

You may have missed it - I very nearly did myself - but Wednesday 28 November marked the 100th Anniversary of the emergence of Albania as an independent nation. OK, Albania may not be a country that makes a loud beep on your international radar. Its population, hovering on either side of three million, depending on which source you look at, undoubtedly ranks it among the minnows of Europe. If you have any mental image of the country at all, chances are it's not awfully positive. Perhaps you've seen the *'Taken'* movies, where ex-CIA agent Liam Neeson single-handedly dispatches an extended family of spectacularly incompetent Albanian bad guys intent on killing him along with his lissom wife and daughter.

Well, I admit it - I do empathise with small countries struggling to make a splash in the ocean of world opinion. Coming as I do from a nation whose population is creeping towards the five million mark, I know what it's like. *'Oh, you come from Auckland - California, right?'* or more commonly, when someone picks the accent, *'So, what part of Australia are you from?'* Perhaps that's another reason I have a soft spot for Turkey. Not that we can compare in terms of land area (about one-third) or population (one-sixteenth), but no one knows much about either of us.

By chance I have a young Albanian colleague at work who proudly informed me of Wednesday's importance in the Albanian national consciousness. I use that phrase because Miranda herself comes from Kosovo, and there is a significant Albanian diaspora in many European and major US cities, who have, apparently, been celebrating somewhat noisily in the past week. Miranda is the second ethnic Albanian I have come to know quite well while living in Istanbul. The other, Dritan, hosted me for a few days on a work-related visit to the Albanian capital Tirana a couple of years ago. I can't say how typical these two are of their race, but I can say they are two of the most intelligent, talented, hard working, sincere and honest young people you could hope to meet. Unlike us New Zealanders, born with the God-given gift of English as our native language, Albanians struggle with the harsh truth that no one much wants to learn their tongue. Perhaps that's why these two seem to have a gift for learning others - French, Italian, English, Serbian, Turkish, Russian . . .

Anyway, as I said, I had the opportunity to visit their beautiful country in January 2010. It's always better to see a new country with a local guide, especially when you don't know the language. Albanian at least belongs to the Indo-European family, which perhaps makes it easier for us than Turkish - but I didn't pick up much in my three days there, apart from learning that 'Albania' bears no resemblance whatsoever to the word the natives use for their own country: *Shqiperie!* Still, the Germans have to put up with us calling them 'Germans', so they're in good company I guess. But not to digress, Dritan and his family made me wonderfully welcome, and I had the opportunity to see three cities, Tirana itself, Shkodra and Vlore.

Dip into travel books and websites about Albania; you'll find they all mention the scenic beauty, the mountains, beaches . . . and the flora and fauna, which apparently represent one of the last remnants of primeval Europe, its extensive forests providing habitats for wolves, bears, the almost extinct European lynx, and the golden eagle, Albania's national symbol.

Well, I'm proud of our kiwi, of course, but an eagle is something else, isn't it! Still, that's another thing we New Zealanders have in common with Albania - a small population and minimal industrial development have some advantages in terms of preserving nature. Two of my enduring memories of the country, apart from the marvellous hospitality of the people, are of the majestic mountains. My first sight of them was as my plane approached Tirana from the Adriatic coast. And later, dining with my hosts at a restaurant beside Lake Shkodra as a full moon rose behind snow-capped peaks on the far shore, turning the still waters to a sea of silver.

As my grandmother used to tell us kids, every cloud is lined with silver, and its natural beauties must be the silver lining for a country that has had more than its share of cloud cover over the years. Albania achieved independent statehood in 1912 as the Ottoman Empire was entering its last years, but if its people had thought they would be left alone to determine their own destiny, they were to be sorely disappointed. Like their neighbour Greece eighty years previously, they were thoughtfully provided with a king from the extensive aristocracy of Germany - William of Vied. During the First World War they were invaded by Greece and later by Italy, regaining independence for another spell in the 1920s and 30s, when a gentleman by the name of Ahmet Bey Zogu seems to have played a pivotal part. This multi-faceted character apparently got himself elected to office once or twice, participated in a couple of military coups on the winning, then the losing side, ending up in a royal role as King Zog the First (to the best of my knowledge, there hasn't been a Zog the Second), before being finally sent packing when Mussolini's Italians mussoled in in 1939. After the Italians surrendered, the Germans moved in till the end of hostilities in 1945. Perhaps these experiences help to explain why Albanians chose a singularly isolationist road of their own in the chaos that enveloped Eastern Europe when peace finally broke out.

Enver Hoxha ruled Albania with the iron hand of ultra-pure communism for forty years until his death in 1985. So pure was his dogma that, in his eyes, post-Stalinist Soviet Russia lacked doctrinal credibility, and he threw in his lot with Red China. The country that, after 1990, emerged blinking into the brave new world of capitalism triumphant, was, as one might imagine, somewhat behind in the trappings of material modernity. Average per capita income is still among the lowest in Europe[43], the urban architecture of Tirana itself has an Eastern bloc austerity, and the beaches are mostly free of five-star hotels and holiday villages – which could, of course, be seen by some as an advantage.

For the present, Albania's independence looks fairly secure. Capitalist development, for better and worse, is under way, and one of the things that struck me in Tirana (apart from the ubiquity of Mercedes Benz motor cars) was the vibrant café scene – a sure sign of post-modern urban sophistication. Other things that caught my attention were the frequency of Turkish Muslim names among the people, and the large mosque occupying a strategic spot in Tirana's main square – reminders that Albania was ruled by the Ottomans for nearly five centuries, from 1431 until the Conference of London brought formal recognition of independence in 1913.

The initial conquest was apparently a protracted process, drawn out by the pugnacious determination of George Kastrioti Skanderbeg, Albania's very own Alexander the Great, who organised resistance to Ottoman military power for thirty-five years, before the end came in 1478. Even then, he might have been successful if the promised assistance from Papal Europe had shown up. Albanian relations with the rest of Europe, it seems, have long been problematic.

Nevertheless, having finally come under Ottoman suzerainty, Albanians seem have taken to their new situation with a will. It is said that more than two dozen Grand Viziers of the Empire were of Albanian extraction, including several members of the Köprülü family, who served with distinction during the glory days of Ottoman power. The majority of their countrymen apparently converted to Islam at this time, which accounts for those names I found familiar on my visit.

---

43 http://en.wikipedia.org/wiki/Economy_of_Albania

But how to account for the name *'Albania'*? Even allowing for our English tendency to mangle unfamiliar words from other languages, it's hard to see how the local name could have been mutilated to that extent. Admittedly, even with a modicum of good will, it's not easy to make an Anglo-Saxon tongue do *'Shqiperie'*. My researches showed that *'Albania'* owes its origins to Medieval Latin, and seems to have been applied fairly indiscriminately to remote places of minimal geopolitical significance. Scotland, the land of my fathers (and mothers) picked up that label at one time in its history – probably around the time when medieval monks had a monopoly on Western education, and were instructing their students that 'here be dragons', and traveling too far in any direction would likely result in your falling off the edge of the world. Anyway, maybe that's another reason I feel empathy for Albanians. If the monks had known about New Zealand in those days, they'd probably have called it Albania too.

Well, I'm sorry I missed the centennial celebrations. If I'd heard in advance, I'd have been tempted to head off to Tirana with a bottle of duty-free whisky and spend the evening with Dritan's family. I'll bet it would have been a good night!

19

Turkish Wine -
Rediscovering an ancient art

6 January 2013

I come from a beer-drinking country. Well, we're not as mono-cultural as we once were, thank God. When I was a kid, New Zealand culture could be pretty much summed up by the three words: Rugby, Racing, and Beer. There was an institution known as *'The 6 O'clock Swill'*. This phenomenon owed its existence to the fact that pubs in NZ used to close their doors at 6 pm, or shortly thereafter. Those who had built up a thirst during their working day (mostly men at that period of our history) had one hour to get to the nearest watering hole and quaff as much ale as they could before the law of the land decreed that they should get out and head home to their loving wives and/or families. As you may imagine, this was not conducive to the development of civilised drinking habits – and the effects are still felt, a generation or two on.

Of course, other alcoholic beverages were available. The more sophisticated or perhaps feminine might sip sherry, or something euphemistically labelled *'Pimms'*. Continental tastes were provided for by immigrants from Eastern Europe, who produced something distantly akin to red wine, commonly referred to as 'Dally Plonk'. Unshaven gentlemen of no fixed abode were sometimes to be seen on park benches sampling this brew from bottles concealed in plain brown paper bags.

I'm happy to say, we are a more civilised nation these days. A referendum in 1967 extended bar hours to 10 pm – allowing for less frenetic speed drinking. Somewhere around the late 1970s, a wine culture started to gain a foothold. Citizens began to discover the surprising fact that moderate consumption of alcohol could accompany a meal and intelligent conversation. The drinks themselves could become a topic for discussion: *"Well, I'd say this full-bodied red shows dark rich berry, chocolate and spice characters enhanced by subtle toasty oak nuances, what would you say darling?" "Oh do shut up, Charles, and pass the bottle, won't you?"*

These days, teachers and civil servants nearing retirement age aspire to establishing a boutique winery in Hawkes Bay or Marlborough, or some other location where the microclimate is conducive and the real estate prices more affordable. New Zealand wines have a well-earned reputation abroad, winning medals at international events, and wine exports are a nice little earner for our humble economy. New Zealanders of a certain class pride themselves, not only on knowing the difference between a Chardonnay and a Sauvignon Blanc, but also on what vintages of which particular vineyards produced the best ones.

What I want to say here is, though, this didn't happen over night. An increasingly wealthy society and an expanding middle class availed themselves of greater opportunities to travel abroad and see for themselves the older oenophile cultures of Europe. Organisations of wine producers brought together like-minded entrepreneurs who exerted persuasive pressure on governments to create a favourable climate for growth, and on the media to help in educating the populace and building a potential market. Another factor has undoubtedly been a hard-line approach by authorities to drivers who drink, such that it is a brave soul who gets behind the steering wheel after even one beer at the pub.

Two generations, then, have seen radical changes in drinking patterns of New Zealanders (and our Australian cousins, though I have to confess, they were always a little ahead of us). These days, executives and other high-flyers watch rugby matches while sipping quality wines in corporate boxes with their spouses or paramours. Of course, remnants of the old ways live on in footie clubs and suburban beer barns - but as a nation, we have diversified in many fields, and alcohol consumption is one measure of this.

So, what about Turkey, you're asking. Weren't you going to say something about that? And so I am. The land occupied by the modern Republic of Turkey is one of the birthplaces of human civilisation. Asia Minor and the plains between the two rivers, whose waters rise in south-eastern Turkey, witnessed the first domestication of animals and the growing of crops for food, the moulding and firing of clay to make pots, and the early stages of metallurgy. Hand in hand with the march of civilisation went the production and consumption of alcoholic beverages. It seems likely that the first wild grapes were cultivated here, and the first hesitant steps taken on the road to producing an award-winning pinot noir. The classical civilisations of Greece and Rome enjoyed their wine. They even assigned responsibility for it to a junior member of their divine pantheon – the Romans, Bacchus, and the Greeks, Dionysus. After the Imperial authorities gave up massacring and otherwise persecuting Christians, and Romans and Greeks joined the ranks of the Saved, apparently they didn't let their new faith stand in the way of imbibing an amphora or two of Bacchus's nectar.

Grape cultivation and wine production in Asia Minor continued in good heart until the Muslim Ottomans took over. The Prophet Muhammed was, I understand, quite specific in his proscription of wine for true believers. Why didn't he mention beer, cider, *Pimms* and other spirituous liquors (if, in fact, he didn't. My Arabic is not up to checking the original text to see what his exact words were)? Well, one reason very likely is that, in the evolution of alcoholic beverages, distillation arrived relatively late on the scene. Scotch whisky may now be regarded as a traditional tipple North o' the Border, but most of the great whisky houses in fact date from the 19th century, as by the way, do most of the clan tartans. Anyway, the Prophet's lack of omniscience on this one left an alcoholic loophole for Turks to slip through. For some at least, obeying the letter of Koranic law and abstaining from wine is enough - and the considerably more powerful rakı, with an alcohol content of forty-five percent, is readily accepted.

It also helped that the Ottomans adopted a tolerant approach to religious minorities within their borders. Jews, Orthodox Greeks and Armenians were not only permitted to observe their religious customs, speak their own languages and educate their children relatively unmolested, they were also allowed to grow their grapes, trample the vintage, ferment, bottle, sell and imbibe the fruit of the vine pretty much according to established practice. More than a few Sultans, most of whom anyway were born to Christian mothers, are reputed to have liked a drop from time to time - and no doubt some of their Muslim subjects saw little harm, occasionally, in joining their Brothers-of-the-Book in a glass or two for friendship's sake.

Nevertheless, it must be true that, for a considerable period, at a time when European civilization was making great strides towards modern alcoholic sophistication (and in other fields too for all I know), wine production within the Ottoman domains failed to keep pace with developments in France, Italy, Germany and so on. When the Ottoman Empire breathed its last and the Turkish Republic came into existence in 1923, its first president, among a host of better known reforms, freed up the production and consumption of spirituous and fermented liquors. While tobacco and spirits were under state monopoly, wine, probably in deference to the status quo, was left in the hands of private producers - though the state did also establish its own vineyards and wineries.

Tezcan Gürkan, owner of *Ganos* wineries in Mürefte, began his career with the state *Tekel* organisation. His vines produce a range of boutique wines, red and white, under the *Krater*, and the more up-market *Ganos* label. Tezcan Bey has mixed feelings about the current state of the wine industry in Turkey. He is passionate about its long history, and its potential to compete in world markets, owing to the country's congenial climate and fertile soils. In terms of human health, he points out, the benefits of moderate wine consumption, especially red wine, in reducing the risk of heart attack, diabetes and even some forms of cancer, have been well publicized. Tezcan Bey further notes that, in the past ten years, during the tenure of the present AK Party government, locally produced wines have improved markedly, both in variety and quality. He is enthusiastic about wines produced from local grape varieties such as *boğazkere*, *öküzgözü* and *kalecik karası*. While accepting that Turkey's climate is more conducive to the production of red wines, he also mentions the potential of *narince* and other white varieties in certain microclimates. On the other hand, he is less sanguine about the future, given the punitive level of taxation targeting alcohol in Turkey. I can attest to this from my own experience, having seen the cost of a mid-price red wine at the supermarket checkout almost double in the past five years.

Still, it's not government policy alone that is impeding the industry's growth. That same bottle of *Angora* or *Villa Doluca*, selling for twenty Turkish liras at *Migros*, will probably add sixty to eighty liras to your bill at a restaurant. The Ministry of Tourism would do well to take a look at the effects of such pricing on visitors to the country. It may be that Turks themselves, weighing up relative value for money, will go for a bottle of rakı with four times the alcohol content - but foreign visitors are more likely to drink one bottle of wine instead of two, and feel scalped into the bargain.

Nevertheless, the younger Gürkan generation seems more optimistic. Tezcan Bey's son, Doruk, recognizes the potential of a growing, and increasingly sophisticated middle class in Turkish cities. One measure of this is the regular appearance these days, of articles in Turkish newspapers and magazines discussing wine, local and imported, and the industry itself. As was the case in my own home country, the twin processes of increasing awareness, and growing demand feed off each other.

Still it is evident that the Turkish wine industry is nowhere near to achieving its potential as an export earner for the nation. A recent article[44] in *Hürriyet* newspaper examined and compared the state of play in a number of comparable countries, in terms of grape vine acreage and wine production. According to their figures, Turkey has the fourth largest area

---

44 http://www.hurriyet.com.tr/yazarlar/22057676.asp

of vines measured by hectares. Only Spain, France and Italy have more grapes under cultivation. In contrast, however, Turkey's wine production is minuscule, at 75 million litres, ranking it way below even New Zealand, with a fraction of the vine acreage. NZ's wine exports, incidentally, generated $868 million of income, and clearly Turkey has the potential to surpass that.

The big problem, as I see it, and Gürkan *pere et fils* among others, apparently agree, is the lack of a large and knowledgeable local market. Whatever the sector, economies of scale determine whether an enterprise will succeed or fail. New Zealand has been able to develop its wine exports because locals drank enough of the stuff to get the business up and running. Turkey, with a population approaching eighty million, had a large enough local market to support the establishment of car manufacturing, electronics and whiteware factories, and a large textile industry - which have then been able to move out into more competitive global markets. New Zealand, unfortunately, with its four-and-a-half million people, lacks this major advantage. Clearly what Turkish wine producers need and seem to lack, is an umbrella organisation that will speak for them, arguing the case for government support of the industry, and engaging in general campaigns to raise public awareness.

As one who enjoys a glass of wine, and appreciates the local product, I'm following developments in the sector with interest.

2 0

Piri Reis's Map – and other big dates in world history

12 January 2013

I don't remember much from my school days, to tell you the truth. I was a moderately successful student, but by no means a hardworking one. I attended French classes for five years, without ever learning to speak or do much else with the language. Perhaps that's the reason I have some sympathy for my Turkish students as they struggle with the mysteries of auxiliary verbs, definite and indefinite articles, and gender-specific 3rd person pronouns. One thing I do have a clear memory of, however, from those five years of French lessons, is a line from the novel *'L'Etranger'* by Albert Camus – *'Je lui ai effleuré les seins'*. The main character, Meursault, is watching a movie at the cinema with a young lady he picks up on the day of his mother's funeral, and he sneaks a quick feel of her breasts, which is what that line says in a slightly more romantic French kind of way.

Well, that may not seem a lot to have learned in five years of studying French, and my old teachers would perhaps be disappointed to hear it - but one thing it has subsequently taught me is never to underestimate the workings of the adolescent male mind. First, you can't know what is going to stick in their febrile brains . . . And second, apart from the elite self-motivated few, if you want to get their attention, you need to keep in mind what sort of things make them tick.

Now you may be wondering why this particular memory chose this particular moment to emerge from my mental synapses, and you may be attributing it to male dotage. However, I can assure you, there is a perfectly valid reason: had he lived, 2013 would have been the year Albert Camus celebrated his 100th birthday. Ok, maybe you're still not with me. How do I know this, you're asking, and why should we care? The fact is I paid a visit to the website of the United Nations Educational Scientific and Cultural Organisation, and I read with interest a list of important historical dates to be observed around the world in the coming year.

For example, it will be 350 years since the death of Nzinga Mbande Ngola Kiluanji, Queen of Matamba-Ndongo in present-day Angola, an *'emblematic figure'*, so the UNESCO people assure me, *'of the struggle against slavery and for women's empowerment in Africa.'* Doctors in Iran and elsewhere will celebrate the 1,000[th] anniversary of the compilation of *'Kitab-al-Qānūn fi ṭ-ṭibb'* by Abd Allah ibn Sina. If that name doesn't mean much to you, you may know him by its Westernised version, Avicenna, the Persian polymath who published his *'Canon of Medicine'* in 1013 CE.

Danish intellectuals, I suppose, and the international community of existentialists, will be gathering in smoke-filled rooms to commemorate the 200th birthday of Sören Kierkegaard, founding father of their movement - and I want to tell you, that happy fact brought back other adolescent memories. For some reason, those writers were in vogue in the days of my youth: Camus, Kierkegaard and close brethren like Jean Paul Sartre, Andre Gide and Samuel Beckett. A lot of them were French, interestingly, and if they weren't, for some reason best known to themselves, they chose to write in that language - which you might think was a commercially poor decision. Another thing they had in common was a preoccupation with the absurdity of human existence - a concept exercising a strange attraction for my youthful male mind on odd occasions when it rose to higher levels of consciousness. Perhaps also, 'absurd' seemed an appropriate description of what we were expected to study at school at a time when the world was on the brink of nuclear annihilation.

Well, it was a few years before I gained a truer appreciation of what those philosophers were on about - that a gut experience of the absurdity of human existence was a stepping stone to personal awareness and ascribing meaning to an individual life - the so-called 'leap of faith'. So maybe you can kind of see why it was important to me - but at the same time, you're still left wondering why I visited that UNESCO website in the first place.

So let me tell you. I'd seen an article in a Turkish newspaper proudly announcing that 2013 would be UNESCO's year of Piri Reis, the 16th century Ottoman cartographer, and I wanted to check it out. In fact, I haven't been able to confirm that the United Nations is/are giving that much importance to Admiral Piri - but he's definitely there on the list, and Turks are proud to claim him as their own. It seems that in 1513, the gentleman in question drew a map, at a time when that particular activity was still in its infancy.

Now, somewhere along the line Turks seem to have lost the art of cartography. In my personal experience, the giving of directions is not a national strong point, and the drawing of a map to help a visitor find their house, an arcane mystery to most. Getting your hands on a document in any way resembling a large-scale topographic map for the purposes of tramping the trackless wastes of Anatolia seems a virtual impossibility. Nevertheless, there was Piri Reis, back around the turn of the 16th century, producing a book entitled *Kitab-ı Bahriye* (*Book of Navigation*), and more especially, a map of the world showing the location of America with remarkable detail and accuracy. According to *Wikipedia*, '*the historical importance of the map lies in its demonstration of the extent of exploration of the New World by approximately 1510, perhaps before others. It used ten Arabian sources, four Indian maps sourced from Portuguese and one map of Columbus.*'

Hacı Ahmet Muhiddin Piri was born sometime in the late 1460s, following his Uncle Kemal into the Ottoman navy, where he seems to have had a long and distinguished career until a ripe old age, winning victories against the Spanish, Venetians and Genoese, helping to conquer Egypt and the Island of Rhodes, and even achieving some successes against the Portuguese around the Persian Gulf and Arabian Coast, in the days before Ottoman sea-power began to wane. After all that you might think a grateful Empire would have awarded a generous pension and sent him into a well earned retirement, but apparently that was not the case. It is to be expected that a chap, even a naval hero of such stature, would be losing a little of his youthful vigour by the time he was in his 80s, but it seems Admiral Piri incurred the wrath of the Ottoman Governor of Basra by refusing to engage in yet another foray against the Portuguese – with the result that said governor had him beheaded in 1553. For sure, life wasn't easy in those days!

But to return to the map, which, you will remember, was our main focus of attention. It seems the Turkish Government back in the 1920s had assigned a German philologist and theologian by the name of Gustav Adolf Deissmann to make a catalogue of non-Islamic items in the library of Topkapı Palace Museum. While engaged in this work, Deissmann turned up, in October 1929, a vellum document of some antiquity, subsequently confirmed to be a fragment of Piri Reis's long lost world map. Knowing that the Ottoman cartographer had used a Columbus map as one of his sources, academics were excited by the prospect that Columbus's original might also be lurking somewhere amongst the Topkapı collection. Sad to say, if it still exists, that source map has yet to be located. However, that was not the only excitement created by Herr Deissmann's find.

Some of my older readers may recall Erich von Daniken, a Swiss gentleman who produced several books back in the late 1960s and early 70s raising the question of whether 'God' had actually been some kind of extra-terrestrial astronaut. Despite the fact that most of his evidence (involving Egyptian pyramids, ancient Peruvians and early Indian stainless steel) has been subsequently discredited, the books still sell well, and Erich von's website claims that he is, in fact, the best-selling non-fiction writer of all time.

His pertinence to our current subject lies in his claim that the Piri Reis map depicted landforms in Antarctica and must have been sourced from documents mapped with advanced technology before the continent was buried under its vast ice sheet. Von Daniken and other 'researchers' of 'palaeo-contact' have made other claims about the map's possible connection to ancient aliens, among them that it: shows the earth as seen from space, shows the sub-glacial topography of Greenland, and is aligned with the earth's 'energy grid'.

Well, I'm not here to discuss the likelihood of alien intervention in human affairs, and the only relevance 2013 has to Erich von Daniken is that it would have been the tenth anniversary of the opening of his theme park near Interlaken in Switzerland, though, unfortunately, it didn't survive to see even its fourth birthday. However, if you're at a loose end, and looking for a new Internet wave to surf, I can recommend that UNESCO list[45] of big dates in world history.

Furthermore, if you do have an interest in UFOs and extra-terrestrial visitations, during my researches I stumbled across these sites that you may like to take a look at: *World Mysteries.com* and *UFO Digest*.

---

45 http://www.unesco.org/new/en/unesco/events/prizes-and-celebrations/celebrations/
anniversaries-celebrated-by-member-states/2013/

21

The Don Draper Syndrome -
More on looted treasures

7 February 2013

There is a popular American TV series, *Mad Men*, set in and around a New York Madison Avenue advertising agency of the 1960s. The central character is charismatic womanizer Don Draper, whose tragic flaw is his shady past. A certain Private Dick Whitman swapped dog tags with, and assumed the identity of his officer, Lt Don Draper, who died alongside him on active service in the Korean War. The reinvented 'Draper' builds a stellar career in the emergent advertising industry, accompanied by his picture postcard wife Betty and their two ideal children.

Well, if you follow the series, you know what I'm talking about and how it turns out – if you don't, it's worth a look, and I'm not going to spoil a fascinating story for you. What I'm really interested in here is the intriguing business of borrowed identity, and its connection to a topic dear to my heart – the treasures of antiquity: who they belong to and what should be done with them.

With a little time to kill in Sydney on my recent trip to see family downnunder, I visited one of the town's lesser-known attractions, the Nicholson

Museum, located on the campus of Sydney University. It's not a huge establishment by world standards, but is said to have the largest collection of antiquities in the Southern Hemisphere. Sydney-siders and Australians generally are indeed fortunate in having access to such a collection of artifacts from Ancient Egypt, Greek and Roman civilizations, and, most interesting to me, a special exhibition showcasing relics of the Etruscans, of whom more later.

Sir Charles Nicholson Baronet was apparently quite a big noise in Sydney back in the mid-19ᵗʰ century. A small plaque near the entrance to the museum informs the visitor that he emerged from humble origins to subsequent fame and fortune – suggesting a fairy tale rags-to-riches, self-made man. A more detailed biography inside explains that Sir Charles had been orphaned as a child and raised by an aunt. The transition from rags to riches had, in fact, been facilitated somewhat by the death of a wealthy uncle who had bequeathed him a substantial fortune.

This fortuitous leg-up set the young man on his path to fame and public honours. He was elected to the New South Wales Legislative Council in 1843, later becoming Speaker of the House. He was one of the founding fathers and first Chancellors of Sydney University and, according to the Australian Dictionary of Biography, was regarded as *'one of the most cultivated men in the colony.'* Financial independence enabled Charles Nicholson to travel extensively through Europe, Egypt and the Near East where, it seems, he amassed *'a large and valuable collection of Egyptian, Roman and Etruscan antiquities'*. One source claims he bought them, which in itself raises interesting questions. This collection he later donated to the University of Sydney, leading to the establishment of the museum that bears his name and preserves it for succeeding generations . . . only it wasn't his name!

Sydney historian Michael Turner, his curiosity aroused, as was mine, by the glib contradictions of the Nicholson fairy tale, carried out a lengthy investigation and established that 'Charles Nicholson' had in fact been born Isaac Ascough in 1808, son of an unmarried maid from a village in Yorkshire. The identity of the father is not known, but clearly there was a mysterious benefactor whose generosity paid for the young Isaac to attend and graduate M.D. from Edinburgh University in 1833. The Ascough uncle, whose legacy provided the wealth for 'Charles Nicholson's' new life, apparently made his pile as owner and captain of ships transporting convicts from the slums of industrial London to the penal colonies of Australia.

The entry in the ADB, on the other hand, reads: *'Sir Charles Nicholson (1808-1903), statesman, landowner, businessman, connoisseur, scholar and physician, was born on 23 November 1808 in Cockermouth, Cumberland, England, the only son of Charles Nicholson, merchant, and of Barbara Ascough, the daughter of a wealthy London merchant'*, and goes on in a similar vein. *Mad Man* Don Draper's transformation pales into small-time insignificance alongside that.

Well, money, like love, is capable of covering a multitude of sins, and charity too, as many a latter-day billionaire will attest. Leaving aside those who acquire it from a lottery ticket, it's a rare human being that can accumulate a major fortune in one lifetime – and an even rarer one who can do it without resorting to shady practices. Having made one's fortune, however, the urge to establish oneself as a pillar of society is strong – and what better way than by donating large sums to a worthy cause or two?

It's mostly speculation on my part, of course. There was nothing illegal about what Uncle Ascough did to accumulate his wealth – the British Government wanted to ship thousands of London's convicted poor to Australia, and getting the shipping contract could be a lucrative business. Still, a sensitive young man might not be too proud of such an uncle and his line of work, even if he inherited the money on said uncle's death. The same sensitive man might also feel twinges of conscience about having 'collected' thousands of priceless antiquities on his Grand Tour of the Ancient World. He might possibly calculate that, with one large donation to the University Museum, he could sanitise the money he had inherited, assuage his conscience, forestall questioning about his origins, and purchase respectability in a new land. I'm not saying that's how it was, but isn't it possible?

Certainly it's not an uncommon practice among the fabulously wealthy. Take George Soros as an example. His *Wikipedia* entry describes him as *'business magnate, investor and philanthropist.'* His philanthropy covers a range of causes, from encouraging democracy in Eastern Europe, through eliminating poverty in Africa, to financing political opposition to the re-election of George W Bush – all worthy objects, you'd have to agree. Mr Soros's wealth, however, was mostly sourced from edgy financial wheeling and dealing, especially currency speculation on a monumental scale. The Prime Minister of Malaysia at the time blamed Soros for the Asian financial collapse of the late 1990s. More recently, he was convicted by French courts for insider trading related to dodgy activities in the late 1980s. One could argue that this Hungarian-American-Jewish 'business magnate' has been one of the prominent engineers of the global financial house of cards that collapsed with such disastrous results for the world economy in 2008.

Of course it's nice, perhaps even praiseworthy that Soros *'gave away over $8 billion to human rights, public health and education causes'* between 1979 and 2011. On the other hand, I imagine he still has a few billion left for his own creature comforts; and if that largesse purchased him a place in heaven and a reputation for philanthropy to go with his honorary doctorates from Yale, Oxford and several lesser universities, he may consider the money to have been well spent.

But I digress. Getting back to the Nicholson Museum in Sydney – its collection includes treasures from Greece, Italy, Egypt and Cyprus. For locals to see such wonders would otherwise require a time-consuming and expensive journey to some Northern Hemisphere institution – so its existence is lucky for Australians. Nevertheless, when you see that monumental sculpted head of Egyptian Pharaoh Rameses II, or the stone capital from a column of the Temple of Bubastis, you can't help marvelling at the achievement of Sir Nicolson-Ascough in getting his collection out of the various countries he visited, and back around the world to Sydney, NSW. For sure, they are not the kind of thing you can stash in a suitcase, conceal in your underwear or secrete in a bodily orifice. We're talking here about some serious manpower, a bullock cart or two, and maybe even a train of camels, not to mention a couple of industrial-size containers. My guess is he didn't have to worry about a 23 kg limit for his check-in baggage on the trip back downunder – but still, it's hard to see the whole enterprise being accomplished without some connivance by local officials who may or may not have been paid off to provide assistance, or at least turn a blind eye.

Undoubtedly regulations regarding the ownership of unearthed antiquities were less stringent in those days, as were those controlling border crossings. At least two books have been published on a phenomenon sometimes known as the *Rape of Egypt*, which reached its peak around the beginning of the 19th century. The passion that overtook genteel Europe has been less offensively referred to as *Egyptomania*, which, however you look at it, involved the mass theft, removal and/or destruction of vast quantities of mummies, statuary and other relics from tombs and pyramids. Apparently there was a fashion in regency drawingrooms for soirées where three or four thousand-year-old corpses were unwrapped for the titillation of the idle rich. Not all were so flagrantly destroyed, however, and one of the sights that impressed me on my visit to the British Museum was a room containing more mummies than I saw in the corresponding institution in Cairo.

To be fair, there is a long tradition of victorious empires uplifting and relocating monuments from conquered territories. The hippodrome in Constantinople contained at least three such trophies, two of which can still be seen in present-day Istanbul: the Serpent Column, originally located in Delphi, Greece; and a huge portion of Egyptian obelisk purloined from the Temple of Karnak, where it had been erected by the Pharaoh Tutmoses around 1400 BCE. The third piece was a group of four bronze horses formerly standing over the entrance to the stadium, which can now be seen adorning the facade of St Marks Basilica in Venice, whither they were transported by knights of the Fourth Crusade after the sack and pillaging of their sister Christian city in 1204. It is said that booty from conquest of Jerusalem in 70 CE financed the building of the Colosseum in Rome by the Emperors Vespasian and Titus – and who remembers that these days?

Two brothers of Italian extraction, Luigi and Alessandro di Palma Ceonola, served sequentially as American consul to Cyprus in the 1860s and 70s. As a sideline to their consular duties, the brothers carried out archaeological excavations, which, after the US ended its diplomatic presence on the island, became a full-time occupation. Their digs resulted in a collection of thousands of valuable artifacts, much of which ended up in the Metropolitan Museum in New York, while some was sold to collectors in the United Kingdom. Authorities in Cyprus today still, I understand, consider the actions of the brothers as tantamount to looting. More recently, another Australian gentleman with the imposing name of Professor James Rivers Barrington Stewart, carried out extensive excavations of burial sites on the island. It was, I gather, only after Cyprus gained independence from Great Britain in 1960 that controls were placed on the removal of ancient artifacts.

I spent a significant portion of my high school days attending classes in the Latin language - for which I am, in fact, quite grateful. In an odd way, its peculiarities of noun declensions, verb conjugations and idiosyncratic syntax prepared me for my later, more practical study of Turkish. Hand in hand with the language, we Grammar boys were also expected to acquire a knowledge of Roman life, history and customs. Not a lot stuck, I have to confess, but I do recall that the Roman calendar was dated from a zero year corresponding to our 753 BCE. Following after the lupine siblings Romulus and Remus, legendary founders of the great city, was a succession of six kings, the last three of which were allegedly Etruscan.

Well, from those days to these, the Etruscans never crossed my path again - until my visit to the Nicholson Museum. That establishment, as I mentioned, houses a collection of relics of those very Etruscans, and I found myself empathising across the millennia with that lost civilization. Very little, it seems, is known of the people whose language and culture were well nigh obliterated by the Romans who conquered them. What we do know mostly derives from tombs and funerary inscriptions, and suggests that Etruscan civilization arose around the 8th century BCE. The people are thought to have originated from Asia Minor, and spoke a language unrelated to any we know.

Professor Graziano Baccolino of the University of Bologna makes the surprising claim that the Etruscans deserve to be recognized as *'the true founders of European civilisation'*, and suggests that the Romans deliberately denied their debt to these people from the East, falsifying their own history to facilitate the cover up. The English novelist DH Lawrence, in a collection of travel essays entitled *'Etruscan Places'*, waxes lyrical on these ancient folk: *'The things* [the Etruscans] *did, in their easy centuries, are as natural and as easy as breathing. They leave the breast breathing freely and pleasantly, with a certain fullness of life. Even the tombs. And that is the true Etruscan quality: ease, naturalness, and an abundance of life, no need to force the mind or the soul in any direction. And death, to the Etruscan, was a pleasant continuance of life, with jewels and wine and flutes playing for the dance. It was neither an ecstasy of bliss, a heaven, nor a purgatory of torment. It was just a natural continuance of the fullness of life. Everything was in terms of life, of living.'*

He is less generous to their conquerors who, he says, *'did wipe out the Etruscan existence as a nation and a people. However, this seems to be the inevitable result of expansion with a big E, which is the sole raison d'étre of people like the Romans.'*

So it's not a new phenomenon. Isaac Ascough aka Sir Charles Nicholson is part of a long tradition wherein sons of empire have, for millennia, appropriated the trappings of overthrown civilisations. Just as inevitable, perhaps, is the emerging trend, in today's world, for descendants of the losing sides to seek redress and perhaps the return of looted treasures. It is not a conflict amenable to easy solution.

22

Redefining Democracy - and getting the monkey off Turkey's back

23 March 2013

I've spent several years trying to define and or describe Turkey and its people in my writings– and now I feel I'm ready to tackle one of the world's really big questions. What is this 'democracy' thing that people keep talking about?

William J Clinton to the contrary, it was the USA's 16th President Abraham Lincoln, in his Gettysburg Address of 1863, who asserted that 750,000 of his citizens would die in the Civil War *'that government of the people, by the people for the people shall not perish from the earth.'* Well, he didn't know the exact figure at that stage, of course, but he must have known it would be a lot. He was, we assume, expressing his support for a democratic system of government, despite the fact that the vast bulk of the US population in those days was not eligible to cast a vote.

The word 'democracy' has a long history, yet as a concept, it has only relatively recently become widely accepted as a desirable goal, and among political leaders, tends to be more honoured in the breach than the observance. Encyclopaedia entries and tourist brochures describing the modern nation of Greece often refer to that land as the cradle of democracy. In truth, however, the much vaunted Athenian system of Cleisthenes lasted a mere two hundred years, more than two and a half millennia ago - and at best allowed for the participation of perhaps twenty percent of the population.

Subsequently, there was not even self-government in that small corner of the Mediterranean until the 19th century when the Great Powers of Europe wrested it from the Ottoman Empire. Even then, self-government is a misleading term, given that said Great Powers installed, first a German, then a Danish Prince on the throne of the kingdom they had created. The foreign-imposed monarchy lasted, on and off, until 1967 when it was finally deposed by a military coup, whose generals ruled the country with an iron fist until 1974. So it seems democracy as a political system has an uncertain, questionable pedigree at best.

Still, it's a worthy aim, for all that. However, you can understand that some might view it with cynicism. Check any collection of quotations on the subject: *'The best argument against democracy is a five-minute conversation with the average voter.'* (Winston Churchill); *'The difference between a democracy and a dictatorship is that in a democracy you vote first and take orders later; in a dictatorship you don't have to waste your time voting.'* (Charles Bukowski).

Apart from the cynics, much of the other wisdom has to do with the fragility of the concept when put into practice, and its vulnerability to abuse and manipulation: *'Democracy cannot succeed unless those who express their choice are prepared to choose wisely. The real safeguard of democracy, therefore, is education.'* (Franklin D. Roosevelt); *'A healthy democracy requires a decent society; it requires that we are honorable, generous, tolerant and respectful.'* (Charles W. Pickering). Education of the masses is seen as an indispensable component, as is constant vigilance, by which we may understand, an effective system of checks and balances – not to mention a need for honest folks in high places, and probably compulsory polygraph testing for lying and hypocrisy, especially in the case of high court judges.

The big problem is that in any country or institution, the ruling elite is always understandably reluctant to surrender its grasp on power. As they are forced to give up concessions to populist reformers - abolition of slavery, universal suffrage (especially for the non-wealthy, and for women), an open press, the secret ballot, objective supervision of vote-counting and so on - they are obliged to find more subtle ways of ensuring that votes cast do not unduly hamper their pursuit of riches and power.

One such method is the sophisticated, expensive and lucrative system of political lobbying. According to *Wikipedia*: '*Wall Street lobbyists and the financial industry spent upwards of $100 million in one year to "court regulators and lawmakers", particularly since they were "finalizing new regulations for lending, trading and debit card fees.". . . . Big banks were "prolific spenders" on lobbying; JPMorgan Chase has an in-house team of lobbyists who spent $3.3 million in 2010; the American Bankers Association spent $4.6 million on lobbying; an organization representing 100 of the nation's largest financial firms called the Financial Services Roundtable spent heavily as well. A trade group representing Hedge Funds spent more than $1 million in one quarter trying to influence the government about financial regulations, including an effort to try to change a rule that might demand greater disclosure requirements for funds.*' Given this level of expenditure, what would you say are the chances of persuading Congress that Wall St needs a little more regulating?

Another method of circumventing the democratic process is the creation of 'flexible' labour markets - which essentially means the removal of manufacturing and service industries from countries with high labour costs (read 'a reasonable standard of living for all') to poor countries where workers can be exploited for wretchedly low wages and conditions. A useful side benefit of this 'flexibility' is a level of 'structural' unemployment in the original country such that those who do have jobs can be frightened into accepting lower pay and reduced conditions.

Parallel to this 'flexible labour market' runs the establishment of a senior management elite with the power to remunerate themselves beyond King Croesus's wildest dreams for their achievements in reducing costs and maximizing profits for their companies. Since most of their work force is either employed for slave-labour wages in distant third world lands, or too frightened and de-unionised to complain, and the unemployed, on the whole, don't have a voice, we don't hear a lot of criticism. There have, admittedly, been protests in France over the salary package of Renault-Nissan

CEO Carlos Ghosn, though even the French government couldn't convince him it was excessive. Reuters[46] reported recently that, *'Ghosn earned €2.79 million euros from Renault in 2011 and €9.92 million from Nissan in its corresponding financial year, making him one of the highest-paid CEOs in France or Japan.'* In the same article, it was noted that, *'Renault is cutting 7,500 jobs over three years . . . and is demanding union concessions on pay, flexibility and working hours in return for guarantees to keep French plants open.'* Interestingly, my Turkish daily reported the other day that Mr Ghosn had agreed to a 30 percent cut in salary if workers in Turkey's Renault plant accepted the company's new contract. Nice to see the developing world fighting back! Still, it must be comforting to know that you can take a 30 percent cut and still make €9.6 million for a year's work, if work is what the gentleman in question actually does.

It seems, for the most part, that corporate CEOs can pretty much do what they like, especially those in the financial sector, who don't have to worry about uppity union representatives from the factory floor. Nevertheless, you can't be absolutely sure some bleeding heart President isn't going to get nervous about the effect all this is having on the morale of the nation as a whole, and start trying to change things. Lobbying alone may not be sufficient. Political campaign funding is a tried and tested means of buying the support of the people's elected representatives. A recent phenomenon, or at least one that has recently been brought to light, is known as *"dark money"*. What we have here is wealthy individuals hiding behind seemingly public-spirited organizations donating large sums to politicians' election campaigns. Huffington Post[47] gives some examples: *'The Karl Rove-founded Crossroads GPS, the Koch brothers' Americans for Prosperity, Grover Norquist's Americans for Tax Reform, the shadowy American Future Fund, and the U.S. Chamber of Commerce have spent $295 million since the beginning of 2011, targeting candidates from President Barack Obama on*

---

46 http://mobile.reuters.com/article/businessNews/idUSBRE90S0L020130129?irpc=932

47 http://www.huffingtonpost.com/2012/11/02/dark-money-2012-election-400-million_n_2065689.html

down to the most contested House and Senate races, all without disclosing the names of their donors to the public.

'These groups are organized as either social welfare non-profits under section 501(c)(4) of the tax code or, in the case of the Chamber of Commerce, as a trade association under section 501(c)(6). Since these groups qualify for tax-exempt status, they are also exempt from disclosing their donors, which political committees are required to do.

'In total, these "dark money" groups have combined to spend $416 million on the 2012 election.'

Once you have these systems in place, you can pretty much guarantee that things will go the way of big business. On the other hand, there remains the problem of investigative news media that may probe and embarrass your tame politicians. It's not a major problem, since your big business probably owns most of the media anyway - but still you may get the occasional maverick. What you really need to do is ensure that your system is so deeply entrenched and unresponsive to uncontrolled influence and change that most of the citizens who might want reform have been effectively disenfranchised. A post-election article in *Time Magazine*[48] noted that large numbers of reporters slaved throughout the presidential campaign to ferret out lies and contradictions perpetrated by candidates:

'Clear examples of deception fill websites, appear on nightly newscasts and run on the front pages of newspapers. But the truth squads have had only marginal success in changing the behavior of the campaigns and almost no impact on the outside groups that peddle unvarnished falsehoods with even less accountability. "We're not going to let our campaign be dictated by fact checkers," explained Neil Newhouse, Romney's pollster, echoing his industry's conventional wisdom.'

---

48 http://swampland.time.com/2012/10/03/blue-truth-red-truth/

Clearly both political party machines are happy to play fast and loose with the truth, secure in the knowledge that the system is stacked against accountability. In consequence, voter turnout in US Presidential elections seems to reflect a lack of belief in the electoral system. It is estimated that 57.5 percent of eligible voters turned out at the polls in 2012. Mitt Romney was ridiculed and lambasted for stating that 47 percent of voters would vote for Obama no matter what, so he didn't have to worry about them. In fact, forty-three percent of US voters, approximately ninety-three million citizens, have been so effectively cut out of the democratic process that neither party needs to think about them.

Which brings me to my next point in the sorry tale of exemplary democracy. Does anyone really understand how representatives are sent to the US Congress and Senate, and how a President is elected? And if they do, can they explain to what extent the results actually reflect the wishes of US voters? The current system for electing a US President was designed by the founding fathers at the birth of the Republic, allegedly to guard against potential evils, one of which was the dominance of party politics. In fact, the same two parties have been taking turns to screw the country for the past 160 years, the 'Democrats' since 1832, and the Republicans since 1854. Interestingly, at the time of Abraham Lincoln's Civil War, the Democrats were actually the pro-slavery party - another bend sinister on the ancestral escutcheon of democracy.

Former First Lady Hillary Clinton is said to have told the European Parliament in 2009[49], *I never understood multi-party democracy. It's hard enough with two parties.* If Madame Clinton actually did utter those words, and if they truly reflect her opinion, you'd have to wonder whether she has the mental equipment to cast a responsible vote, never mind carry out the duties of Secretary of State or, God forbid, President of the most powerful nation on Earth! For Mrs Clinton's information, the majority of the world's democratic states employ a proportional representation electoral system which allows for the presence in their legislative

---

49 http://www.reuters.com/article/2009/03/06/us-eu-clinton-gaffes-idUSTRE5253XS20090306

assemblies of several political parties - and most of those countries have a higher turnout at the polls than the USA. Not surprising when you remember that the media were telling us prior to the 2012 election that, if you didn't live in Florida, Pennsylvania, Michigan, North Carolina, Virginia, Wisconsin, Colorado, Iowa, Ohio, Nevada or New Hampshire, you might as well stay home for all the difference your vote would make to the final result.

One of the things that have impressed me about Turkey in recent years is the capacity for change within the system. When I first came to this country in 1995, the AK Party currently in power did not exist. Now, none of the parties involved in government at that time can manage a single representative in parliament. Very likely, Mrs Clinton would struggle in such an environment. She wouldn't know which lobbyists to listen to, or which unaffiliated public interest group to accept campaign funds from - or even which party to join. The Turkish system may be tough on politicians, financiers and retired army generals, but it does keep Turkish voters interested. And I suspect a good number of those 93 million non-voting Americans would make more effort if there were a little more choice on their voting papers.

Undoubtedly there are social and economic problems in Turkey. The education system is desperately in need of serious expert attention, for instance, and the gulf between rich and poor is unacceptably high. On the other hand, the nation has so far avoided the worst effects of the world financial crisis that has battered its European neighbours Greece, Italy, Spain, Portugal, Ireland and even the UK. The home of modern democracy seems to have silenced its discontented poor for the time being, but tens of thousands have been taking to the streets regularly in the PIIGS nations in recent months to protest their government's imposed 'austerity' measures.

'Austerity', needless to say, is generally understood to mean reducing pensions and social welfare benefits for the retired and unemployed, cutting back the public sector workforce, and reducing spending on education and public health. Little in the way of belt-tightening is required from the banking and finance sectors – Irish banks, for example, have reportedly received €64 billion in government handouts to keep them solvent. Furthermore, those government handouts are funded from tax paid by the diminishing pool of wage and salary earners, or more likely, given their indebtedness, by government borrowing from banks. In the mean time, the UK parliament has published a report announcing plans to try and collect billions of pounds in tax from US multinational corporations such as *Starbucks*, *Google* and *Amazon*, who use a technique referred to as 'profit-shifting' to pretty much avoid paying any tax at all. The *New York Times* reported[50] the other day that, '*Starbucks said . . . that it was reviewing its British tax practices after the company disclosed recently that it had paid no corporate tax in Britain last year despite generating £398 million in sales.*' Unfortunately, the article goes on to say, the British Government expects that their campaign to extract a little internal revenue from these sources will cost them at least £77 million.

Still, the British taxpayer has got it soft compared to his or her American counterpart. According to a recent article in *Time*, the Pentagon is splashing out $400 billion dollars to purchase 2,457 Lockheed F-35 fighters that are apparently starting to show many of the attributes of a white elephant. At approximately $160 million each, the single-seat warplane costs about the same as a 204-seater Boeing 767. I don't remember seeing that voters were offered the opportunity to say yay or nay to this project in last year's national presidential poll – but I suspect not. The same article quotes a Republican senator saying that US spending on 'defence' now accounts for 45 percent of the world's total.

Well, so much for the power of a democratically exercised vote, and the fair spread of the tax burden over those able to pay. What about equality before the law, another foundation stone of a democratic system? A recent study carried out in New Zealand by an academic at Victoria University found that white-collar fraudsters are far less likely to spend time in jail than denizens of society's lower echelons hauled into court for welfare ben-

---

50 http://www.nytimes.com/2012/12/04/business/global/british-lawmakers-accuse-mulitna-tionals-of-immorally-avoiding-taxes.html?_r=0

efit cheating – in spite of the fact that the sums of money involved are invariably much larger in the former group.

Like me, you may be following the case of Jesse Jackson Jr, former Chicago Democrat congressman *once talked about as having the potential to become the first black president*[51], who has admitted charges of channelling campaign funds to his personal use. Apparently Jesse Jr delegated the responsibility for the family tax forms to his wife Sandi, a Chicago City Councillor – who is also facing charges for filing false returns. Let's see what happens to them, bearing in mind that a blue-collar employee who steals from his or her employer is usually treated harshly by the justice system. And then there is Dominique Strauss-Kahn, former IMF chief with plans to run for President of France. His stellar career was derailed when a hotel maid accused him of sexual assault. Strauss-Kahn's lawyers were able to discredit the woman and avoid criminal prosecution, but she subsequently brought a civil case against him. The latest news is that the case has been settled out of court for an undisclosed, but presumably large sum. Well, you'd have to wonder why the guy would want to do that if he was, in fact, innocent. You can't help feeling that Big Abe's famous words could be modified these days to: Government of the people by a small and privileged elite largely for the benefit of that latter group. Monsieur Dominique, incidentally, would have been standing as a Socialist candidate!

Anyway, where does all that leave us? I'm sure you knew or suspected most of the foregoing, even if you may not have known all the fine details. I fondly remember the days when my own name was on the ballot paper in New Zealand, which made casting a vote in national elections so much easier. These days it seems I don't qualify to exercise democratic voting rights in New Zealand or Turkey, so for the most part, I just sit on the sidelines and offer helpful comments. Still, I do feel that the Western media should assist in getting their own national houses in order before criticising too harshly democracy in Turkey and elsewhere.

---

51 http://www.huffingtonpost.com/2013/02/15/jesse-jackson-jr-guilty-plea_n_2698769.html

23

The Obscenity of Extreme Wealth

16 March 2013

"The gap between rich and poor in OECD countries has reached its highest level for over 30 years, and governments must act quickly to tackle inequality, according to a new OECD report."[52] Well, that report was released in December 2011. I haven't seen a recent update, and I don't know what's happening in your particular part of the world – but from a purely empirical point-of-view, I'd say governments are dragging their feet on this one.

The OECD uses something called the *Gini* Coefficient to graph inequality in twenty-two countries. Now I have to confess I checked out the *'Gini'* coefficient and gave up trying to understand the maths of it. Still, one thing is clear: in 1985, Mexico and Turkey led the OECD countries in the extent of the gap between rich and poor; while Sweden and Finland, as we might expect, were tops for relative equality.

On the other hand, things had changed by 2008, when the global financial crisis struck. Not surprisingly, the income gap had widened in

---

52 http://www.equalitytrust.org.uk/news/record-inequality-between-rich-and-poor-watch-oecd-video

eighteen of the twenty-two countries – something most of us felt intuitively, if we lacked hard statistical evidence to back up our gut feeling.

"*OECD Secretary-General Angel Gurría said, 'This study dispels the assumptions that the benefits of economic growth will automatically trickle down to the disadvantaged and that greater inequality fosters greater social mobility.'*

"*The main driver behind rising income gaps has been greater inequality in wages and salaries, as the high-skilled have benefitted more from technological progress than the low-skilled. Reforms to boost competition and to make labour markets more adaptable, for example by promoting part-time work or more flexible hours, have promoted productivity and brought more people into work, especially women and low-paid workers. But the rise in part-time and low-paid work also extended the wage gap.*

"*Benefits levels fell in nearly all OECD countries, eligibility rules were tightened to contain spending on social protection, and transfers to the poorest failed to keep pace with earnings growth.*

"*Another factor has been a cut in top tax rates for high-earners. The OECD underlines the need for governments to review their tax systems to ensure that wealthier individuals contribute their fair share of the tax burden. This can be achieved by raising marginal tax rates on the rich but also improving tax compliance, eliminating tax deductions, and reassessing the role of taxes in all forms of property and wealth.*"

Well, nothing very new or revolutionary there. The only really surprising thing is that those at the top-end of the income spectrum keep hogging an obscene share of the world's wealth, and flaunting it with seeming impunity in the faces of the have-nots.

I recently came across a helpful website for those of you whose disposable income has grown to the embarrassing point where you don't know what to do with it: howtospendit.ft.com

It's a kind of *Lonely Planet* guide to shopping for the ludicrously wealthy. If you're looking for something smart in men's shoes, you could do worse than check out JM Weston. Their *Flore 529* in black lizard skin will help you get rid of £1,775. Still some slack in your shoe budget? What the hell, get a second pair. In need of a watch? Hard to go past the *Christophe Claret Soprano Tourbillon* with a price tag of £380,400. You'll find useful links to specialised sites too, where you can pick up, for instance, a nice 750 ml bottle of *Courvoisier L'Esprit* Champagne cognac for $9,300. Included in the price, apparently, is a hand-cut *Lalique* crystal decanter. For those with a taste for jewellery and a sensitive conscience, Karen Ellison, founder of *Jewels For Humanity*, will be happy to help you out. You can relax as you attach your $6,600 cufflinks, clip on your $18,000 earrings, or slip that $185,000 *Sea Treasure Octopus* ring over your pinkie, knowing that twenty percent of your dollars will go to a charity of your choice, *Diamond-miners Without Borders*, for example.

Perhaps your interests run more towards the masculine. Check out Swedish gun and rifle maker VO Vapen. Viggo Olsson, I'm told, constructs the world's most exclusive handmade hunting rifles. If money's no object, there's the H.H. Sheikh Zayed Bin Sultan Al Nahyan Mosque Rifle, priced at $825,000. If you don't need a rifle when you go to the mosque, a more economical purchase would be the "Big Papa" at $375,000; or something from the Viking Collection, inspired by Viking mythology and featuring engravings of Norse gods and 24-carat gold inlay at $275,000 apiece. If you're a little hard up at present, you can pick up a gat from the Royal TD Collection, initially created for H.R.H. Prince Carl Philip Bernadotte of Sweden for a very reasonable $125,000.

To buy a car, though, you really need to get along to a good motor show, such as the one in Geneva, Switzerland. Top of the line this year was the Lamborghini Veneno with a price tag of $US3.9 million. Looking for something hot but just a little cheaper? The new beast from Ferrari may suit. Listed at €1.2 million ($1.62 million), the *F150* has a top speed of 370 km/h, and will accelerate from 0-100 km/h in a little under three seconds. The word is that only five hundred will be manufactured and purchase will be by invitation only. Colour choice is *Rosso Corsa, Giallo Modena* or *Nero,* and if you have to ask what they are, you're probably not on the list.

Obviously you can't consider yourself seriously wealthy without a cellar of vintage wine, and those in the know will send their buyer along to Harrods with the aim of picking up a 'vertical' of *Chateau d'Yquem* for around £1 million. Alternatively, folks with an eye for a bargain might chance on a privately assembled antique collection from Christie's for a similar outlay. I gather the *Yquem* people maintain their exclusivity by limiting their output, and in fact, in some years, 2012 for example, not producing a vintage at all. 2010, on the other hand, was apparently a good year. Expect to pay around £5,000 for a case of twelve bottles.

Still, you can't be quaffing champagne cognac and vintage wine all the time. Sometimes you just need a coffee, right? No need to rub shoulders with the proles in Starbucks though. *Black Ivory* is said to be the world's most exclusive brew, and you can enjoy it, for around $US50 a cup, at the Anantara Dhigu Resort and a couple of other spas in the Maldives, as well as two hotels in Thailand and another pair in Abu Dhabi. If you prefer to brew your own at home, a kilo of the stuff sells for $1,100, hand-cut *Lalique* crystal coffee pot not included. What's the deal, you may ask. It's only coffee, right? Maybe so, but these beans have been passed lovingly through the digestive system of Thai elephants, collected (and carefully washed, we hope) by local women before being packaged and brought to your hotel.

Ah those Arabs! Seems the Muslims are getting the last laugh after all. And what are they doing with the money rolling in from elephant dung coffee and petro-dollars borrowed from China to maintain that non-negotiable American way-of-life? I don't want to burden you with unnecessary details, but, as a sample, take a look at the yacht *'Dubai'* owned by Mohammed Rashid Al Maktoum, Prime Minister and Vice President of the United Arab Emirates, and 'constitutional monarch' of Dubai. That mother, at 162 metres, is the second largest privately owned yacht in the world (come on, Mo, only the second largest?).

Dubai's luxurious interior design blends bold colours with fine fabrics and in-tricately detailed handmade mosaics. A spectacular staircase creates the yacht's showpiece. Bathed in natural light from the top deck, this dramatic circular staircase features glass steps, which change colour. Dubai's spacious decks offer a split-level owner's deck; a large social area including the main lounge with its centrepiece red sofa; numerous VIP and guest suites, and a crew area to accommodate 115 people including crew and guest staff.

With seven decks, Dubai has a wealth of sunbathing areas; a striking mosaic swimming pool and several Jacuzzis. She can accommodate a helicopter of up to 9.5 tonnes and can carry two 10-metre long tenders. Dubai has a displacement of 9,150 tonnes, yet can reach an impressive 26 knots at maximum speed. She has exceptional worldwide capability with a range of 8,500 miles at 25 knots, powered by four MTU diesel engines.

According to superyachts.com, eight of the world's nine largest private yachts are owned by Arabs. But it's not just about yachts. Last summer in Bodrum we were honoured by a visit from Saudi Prince El Velid bin Abdülaziz bin Suud. Well, he didn't actually stay at our place, of course. He had a yacht anchored offshore for him and his family while they were in town, but they flew in on their private plane, which, incidentally, is not one of your piffling Learjets, but a full-size Boeing 747. It's a competitive business, being that rich – don't think it's all plain-sailing. Sultan Haji Hassanal Bolkiah Mu'izaddin Wadaulah ibni Al-Marhum Sultan Haji Omar Ali Saifuddien Sa'adul Khairi Waddien, aka the Sultan, Prime Minister and Yang Di-Pertuan of Brunei, pretty much sets the standard here for others to follow, with his customised Boeing 747-400 and Airbus 340-200. Hassanal Bolkiah (you can call him that if you're short of time) is reputed to have a collection of over 7,000 high performance cars, including 600 Rolls Royces, 300 Ferraris, not to mention assorted Koenigseggs, McLarens, Porsches and other lesser makes.

You probably knew that London's premier department store Harrods is owned by the royal family of Qatar. Seems they bought it on spec a year or two ago, then a gang of them turned up to check it out in a Lamborghini Murcielago LP670-4 Super Veloce and a customised Koenigsegg CCXR, which they parked on the road outside. Apparently while they were in the store, the egalitarian London Constabulary had the vehicles clamped, so once again the Brits have cause to feel proud of their local bobbies.

Nevertheless, like me, you may be starting to feel a little ashamed of your Western Caucasian Anglo-Saxon Christian brothers and sisters, and to think that somebody, somewhere must be letting the side down. So it's heartening to know we have people like Petra Ecclestone going in to bat for our side. Ok, I know she's only the daughter of a rich guy, but you can't blame a girl for that. And besides, knowing that can give us a better appreciation of the league daddy himself is playing in. Bernie has one other daughter besides young Petra, and we must assume he is not leaving her penniless. Clearly, though, Petra is daddy's pet, which is why he bought her that mega-mansion in Los Angeles for $85,000,000, said to be the world's most expensive house. Petra and her husband Jim apparently find the 5700m² chateau 'quite cosy', especially after two months of extensive renovations which, we may guess, added a few millions more to the original purchase price. My invitation to their wedding evidently got lost in the mail, but it must have been quite a bash, seeing as it cost daddy £5 million. Petra herself would have looked lovely too, I'm sure, in her £80,000 dress. Maybe she'll pass it on to her own daughter, when the time comes, for economy's sake.

But you don't have to be an heiress, an Arab Sheikh or a Grand Prix mogul to play in the big league. Wage and salary earners (some of them at least) are doing all right these days too. Take Muhtar Kent, for example, the Turkish CEO of the Coca Cola Company. His 'compensation' last year was a little under $26 million, down a couple of millions from the previous year, but still competitive. I have to say I never touch that black fizzy stuff, preferring, as I do, *Courvoisier L'Esprit*. And I avoid their *Turkuaz* brand bottled water - but I will confess I am partial to their 100 percent *Cappy* Orange Juice, so I feel I have, in some small measure, contributed to the maintenance of Mr Kent's life style.

And now that we have established a Turkish connection, I want to mention our very own construction magnate Ali Ağaoğlu, who dropped into the recent Istanbul Motor Show in his Rolls Royce Phantom Cabrio, reportedly the same model British Queen Elizabeth uses for her shopping expeditions. Strolling around the exhibits, Mr Ağaoğlu's eye was apparently caught by a bright yellow (or *giallo diarrea*, if you prefer) Bugatti Veyron 16.4 Grand Sport, retailing locally for €4.3 million. Looking to fill a gap in his stable of fourteen luxury vehicles, Mr A remarked casually that he might buy one. Can't confirm whether he actually did or not.

Well, if you're not totally nauseated by now, glowing emerald green with envy, or filling out an application form to join your local chapter of Anarchist Bombers Incorporated, let me finish the job I have started. A recent news item under the heading *'Victoria's Dirty Secret'* claimed that the billion dollar creator of up-market frillies imports much of its raw material from the impoverished African nation of Burkino Faso, where children as young as ten are picking cotton without pay, motivated mostly by fear of the beating they will get if they slacken their pace. Needless to say, a spokesperson (not actually Victoria herself) assured reporters that such practices were strictly contrary to company policy - though stopping short of outright denial. And this, it seems to me, is an aspect of the problem that the OECD commentator above touched on. Adaptable/flexible labour markets these days are lubricated by the outsourcing of factories and suppliers of raw materials to third world countries where labour costs are low because of less stringent (or non-existent) laws protecting worker pay and conditions. Implicit in this is the sad fact that companies using these methods of lowering costs do not care about the welfare of those doing the work – they merely want to know the price of the labour. Maybe Posh Spice truly doesn't know about those kids in Burkino Faso – but if she really wanted to, she could surely find out.

The other effect of moving labour costs abroad is that you reduce the need for those jobs in your own country, creating a level of systemic unemployment which ensures that those workers with jobs, desperate to keep them, will accept lower pay and reduced conditions. Does anyone still believe in the trickle-down theory of wealth? How much do you think those Thai women earn for picking coffee beans out of elephant droppings so that the obscenely rich can sip their *Black Ivory* espresso at an exclusive desert resort in Abu Dhabi? Closer to the booming Dow Jones, my latest *Time* informs me that an average of 50,000 people a night slept in New York city's shelters for the homeless in January this year. At least Turkey's Gini Coefficient is down a little – which means the gap between rich and poor has shrunk since 1985. There's still work to be done, but it's a move in the right direction.

24

Tulips From Istanbul

13 April 2013

Spring is a beautiful season in Turkey. The weather is not necessarily all you might wish, but when it's good, it's very, very good. Even the concrete megalopolis of Istanbul puts on a fine show, as trees break into blossom and green leaf. For the last seven years the Metropolitan Council has sponsored a tulip festival in April – this year is the 8th annual event, and according to reports, 14.5 million bulbs of 270 different varieties have been planted in parks, verges and median strips around the city.

Apart from the spectacular colour the blooms are bringing to the lives of city-dwellers, the project must have created employment for a goodly number of nursery-workers, gardeners, drivers, landscape designers, manufacturers of irrigation systems, middle managers and who knows what other peripheral occupations. There are even new opportunities for museum curators and academics. One feature of this year's festival has been the establishment of a tulip museum in Emirgan Park beside the Bosporus on the European side of the city – with funding provided for research.

Turkey's wild flowers have an international reputation amongst those in the know. Apart from the deep layers of history, sites connected with the early development of Christianity and the glory days of Islamic civilisation, tourists visit Turkey, especially in spring, for its natural wonders, particularly the beauties of its endemic flora. Poppies, pansies, daisies, primroses, crocuses and a myriad other wildflowers grow in abundance and turn on vivid displays in this season. Most commonly cultivated tulips, I am told, derive from the genus *tulipa gesneriana*, which grows naturally in Turkey, and was brought to Europe from the Ottoman Empire in the 16th century.

It's an interesting plant, the tulip. Much of its dazzling colour variety, apparently, is the result of a disease, a non-fatal virus - a kind of benign tulip version of yellow or scarlet fever, perhaps. While some people have an allergic reaction to the leaves and petals, tulip bulbs, it seems, can be eaten in safety. They can, in fact, be dried, pulverised and used to make a kind of bread, as, I understand, some Dutch people were obliged to do during the dark days of the Second World War. The flavour, however, was not sufficiently appealing for the practice to catch on, and most Dutch citizens these days prefer to admire the flowers and eat bread from the local *bakkerij*. Nevertheless, some insist that a petal or two adds a little *je ne sais quoi to* a fresh salad, and true aficionados claim to have made an acceptable tulip wine.

Not the Ottomans, though, as far as I can learn. Wine drinking is generally frowned on in traditional Muslim societies, and, while the upper echelons of society may have fancied a drop from time to time, they tended to stick with the grape variety, the vine being also native to the region, and its fruit in plentiful supply.

The word 'tulip' itself comes to us from the Persian language via Ottoman Turkish. Somewhat perversely, we didn't borrow their word for the actual plant and flower, which is *'lale'* in both languages. What we got was the Persian word for a turban, that wended its way slowly through several European tongues like Italian and French, mutated and deformed as it went - in a process similar to that undergone by our word 'mosque'. In Persia, the tulip was intimately bound up in art and literature with romantic love and passion, especially of the unrequited kind - a theme also much admired in Turkish tradition. Islamic societies tended to avoid depicting the human form, or even animals - a prohibition attributed to reaction against the Orthodox Christian practice of kissing and praying to pictures and statues, which Muslims viewed as idolatry. As a result, Islamic art makes much use of geometric designs and stylised floral patterns. The Ottoman ceramic tiles and porcelain ware that reached their highest form in the 16th and 17th centuries often featured tulips, along with carnations, roses and daisies. In recent years the art of marbling (*ebru*) has experienced a resurgence of popularity, with those floral motifs being incorporated into the traditional swirling patterns.

It is not known for certain who first introduced the tulip to Western Europe. It is known, however, that the flower was a gift from the Ottomans, as were coffee, Turkish carpets and the art of making fine porcelain. Two gentlemen in particular tend to receive credit for the introduction. The first is Ogier Ghislain de Busbecq, a Frenchman who served as ambassador from Ferdinand I to the court of Suleiman the Magnificent in the mid-16th century. Now I know it's not strictly relevant, but I just have to tell you about Ferdinand. He was born in Spain to an interesting couple referred to by historians as Joanna the Mad and Phillip the Handsome (so I guess she wasn't that mad). Ferdinand himself compiled an impressive CV during his life, holding, at various times, the titles of Archduke of Austria, King of Bavaria and Hungary, King of the Romans and Holy Roman Emperor.

But getting back to de Busbecq, he was apparently a man of eclectic interests, renowned as one of the pioneers of travel literature, compiling a vocabulary of an obscure Germanic dialect known as Crimean Gothic, and turning up lost gems of classical literature while rummaging through Ottoman libraries. He was fascinated by Anatolian flora and fauna, and sent tulip bulbs to his friend Charles l'Ecluse, a doctor employed in the service of the Habsburg Emperor, Maximilian II. L'Ecluse succeeded in getting the bulbs to grow, first in Vienna, and later, after, after taking up a post as professor at Leiden University in 1593, in the Netherlands.

Tulips were an instant hit in Holland. The Dutch seem to have a knack for growing unlikely plants in their inhospitable northern clime. I learnt recently that they have supplanted Spain as Europe's largest exporter of tomatoes; and I hear plans are afoot to take over the supply of bananas from Ecuador, with large-scale production of pineapples and coconuts to follow. But I digress. We were discussing the popularity of tulips in the Netherlands in the late 16th century, and indeed, so popular were they that, by 1637 they had resulted in a major financial crisis - a classic 'bubble' that later became a case study much loved by students of the 'dismal science'.

The story goes that popularity of and demand for tulip bulbs caused the price to rise in proportion to their scarcity on the market. Entrepreneurs with an eye for a fast guilder moved out of other less lucrative operations (such as selling marijuana in the days before the Dutch legalised it) into the tulip bulb business. Inevitably, stockpiling occurred, and soon a bustling futures market developed, with prices skyrocketing to unimaginable heights – at least to primitive folk unaccustomed to dotcom booms and suchlike phenomena characteristic of more advanced civilisations. At the peak of *tulipmania* the price of a bulb increased twenty-fold in a month. Some speculators were selling up their worldly possessions to invest in tulips and make their fortunes. One optimistic soul is reputed to have exchanged *'two lasts of wheat, four lasts of rye, four fat oxen, eight fat swine, twelve fat sheep, two hogsheads of wine, four tuns of beer, two tons of butter, 1,000 lb. of cheese, a complete bed, a suit of clothes and a silver drinking cup'* for one particularly desirable bulb.

Well, as you might have expected, it all ended in tears, certainly for those who failed to get out in time. The 'bubble' burst in the winter of 1636-7, many investors lost their shirts, not to mention their beds, swine and hogsheads, and the economy was thrown into depression for several years. The Dutch continued to love tulips, albeit in moderation, and learnt a healthy respect for the dangers of speculative 'bubbles'.

The Ottomans, meanwhile continued to paint pictures of tulips inside the domes of their mosques, and secretly present yellow blooms to beloveds who would never love them back, in an altogether more restrained fashion. That all changed, however, on the accession of Sultan Ahmet III in 1718. The next twenty-two years are known in Ottoman history as *Lale Devri* ('The Tulip Age'), a time when the social elite adopted the tulip as its symbol of status and wealth. Ahmet is an interesting example of the cosmopolitan nature of Ottoman society, born in Dobruja, on the border between modern Bulgaria and Romania, his mother being an ethnic Greek, and his two wives, French. His reign was also a time when the Ottomans began adopting an openness towards Europe, perhaps recognising that their own greatest days of glory were in the past. Nevertheless, Ahmet was the last Ottoman Sultan to have significant military success against Russia – and during his reign the printing press was belatedly employed for the production of books in Ottoman Turkish. Imperial architecture underwent a major change at this time with the adoption of baroque influences on mosques and other monumental buildings. One of my favourite mosques in Istanbul is Yeni Valide Camii, which was built for Ahmet's mother in the seaside township of Üsküdar on the Asian coast of the Bosporus.

I can't leave this discussion here, because I know I will once again be criticised for pro-Turkish, pro-Muslim favouritism, so I'm going to share with you a little snippet of information I learnt about my Christian forebears, in particular, John Calvin, one of the key figures in the Protestant Reformation of the 16th century. His doctrine, known as *Calvinism*, underpins the Presbyterian Church among others, and its main principles can be recalled to mind by use of the simple mnemonic TULIP:

T – for *Total Depravity*, which means we are all sunk deep in sin and cannot save ourselves from hell and damnation.

U – for *Unconditional Election*, which means that God has already decided who He's going to save, and nothing you or I can do will change His Divine decision.

L – *Limited Atonement*. Essentially, Jesus died for us sinners, but only those on God's special list will get the benefit.

I – *Irresistible Grace*. If you're on that list, God's gonna get you, whether you want to be saved or not.

P – *Perseverance of the Saints* – If you're on that list, you're on it for good and all. Do what you like, you can't get off it.

Well, I don't know about you, but it seems to me if you believe in **TULIP**, you're living in a pretty fragile glasshouse, and you'd better not throw stones at anyone else's religious beliefs.

To end on a more positive note, if you get along to that museum during this year's Istanbul Tulip Festival, you can download an app on your smart phone that will read barcodes on the blooms and identify their names and special features. If you leave your address with the organisers, I'm told they will send you a tulip bulb. No lasts of rye or tuns of beer required – just free, gratis and for nothing.

25

Ding Dong. Who's There?
A Witch and a Wizard

18 April 2013

A *Facebook* group had, it seems, been planning for several years to make *'Ding Dong the Witch is Dead'*, from the 1939 film *'The Wizard of Oz'*, No 1 song in the UK when Margaret Thatcher died. I have no idea what's topping the charts in Venezuela these days, because I've been busy marking student essays at the university where I work. Maybe that's what did it. An essay topic insinuated itself into my brain, and like the Ancient Mariner's woeful agony, wouldn't leave me alone until I'd buttonholed you and shared my tale, so here it is:

'Compare and contrast the lives and political careers of Hugo Chavez and Margaret Thatcher'

The world lost two colourful and controversial political figures in 2013. Both had served long terms as leader of their countries: Hugo Chavez as President of Venezuela for fourteen years; Margaret Thatcher as Prime Minister of Britain for almost twelve.

Both leaders divided their nations into dramatically polarised groups - those who loved them and those who hated and detested them. Both achieved considerable international recognition during their lifetime. *Time* ranked Chavez among the world's *'100 Most Influential People'* in 2005 and 2006. The same weekly had Thatcher in its *'100 Most Important People of the 20th Century'*. The British magazine *New Statesman* (admittedly leftist) placed Chavez eleventh on their list of *'Heroes of Our Time'*. A BBC poll to find the *'100 Greatest Britons'* had Dame Maggie at number sixteen on the list – a ranking somewhat devalued, I fear, by its having Princess Diana in third place.

Thatcher is said to be the only post-war Oxford-educated PM not to have been awarded an honorary doctorate by her alma mater. Chavez on the other hand received several such awards, from universities as far away as South Korea, Russia and Beijing.

Both were ideologues, committed to particular, somewhat extreme political doctrines which they single-mindedly applied in the face of strong opposition: Thatcher to the monetarism of Milton Friedman, and Chavez to socialism and populism, and his revolutionary heroes, Simon Bolivar and Che Guevara.

Both formed strong bonds with like-minded leaders on the international stage: Thatcher with US presidents Ronald Reagan and George Bush the Father, Chilean military dictator Augusto Pinochet and the Prime Minister of apartheid-era South Africa, PW Botha; Chavez with South American neighbours Fidel Castro and Rafael Correa, and Iranian president Mahmud Ahmedinejad.

Thatcher crushed the unions, broke down the traditions of collective workplace bargaining, championed an individualistic, free-market privatised economy where financiers were given free reign, and paved the way for a new society with summers of content for the wealthy and an underclass tucked away out of sight, occasionally rising in disorganised protest and ruthlessly suppressed. British Labour MP Glenda Jackson, speaking in a parliamentary debate[53]

---

53 http://www.opendemocracy.net/ourkingdom/glenda-jackson/thatcher-woman-not-on-my-terms

after Thatcher's death, described that lady's achievement as *'the most heinous social, economic and spiritual damage upon this country.'*

Chavez took on the problems of poverty and slums associated with un-controlled urbanisation, addressed the evils of inadequate food production and profiteering, and reduced poverty in Venezuela from 59 to 24 percent of the population. He was the leader of a South American nation strug-gling with the legacy of colonialism, corruption, large-scale poverty and huge inequalities of wealth distribution.

Thatcher, on the other hand, headed a West European country with a history of imperialist and colonial exploitation, and the sixth largest econo-my in the world, who went to war with a much poorer and technologically inferior South American state to preserve her nation's right to own a tiny island in the South Atlantic Ocean 12,500 km from its own shores. Cynics have suggested that, if not for the wave of jingoistic patriotism and media frenzy generated by this ten-week mini-war, Thatcher might have been a one-term rather than a three-term Prime Minster. Even her first election victory, in 1979, was achieved with the support of former National Front voters, who deserted their far right nationalist whites-only party to side with the 'Iron Lady'.

Both premiers came from relatively humble origins – Thatcher, daugh-ter of a Grantham grocer, who did, though, own two stores; Chavez born to small-town working class parents. Margaret Hilda Roberts, however was able to marry a millionaire businessman, Denis Thatcher, who financed her through law school (after her first career as a chemist foundered), sup-ported her in her early political career, and purchased their two comfort-able homes, in Chelsea and rural Kent. In an interview in 1970, Hubby Thatcher is quoted as saying, *'I don't pretend that I'm anything but an hon-est-to-God right-winger – those are my views and I don't care who knows 'em'.* Funny how those right-wing loonies always seem to find a way to bring God in on their side. Maggie's father-in-law, incidentally, was apparently born in New Zealand, so I and my fellow Kiwis can claim some interest in the Baroness's rise to power.

The Venezuelan leader died in office after a battle with cancer, still popu-lar enough in his own country to have been re-elected to a fourth term as president in 2012. The dear departed Briton was more or less obliged to resign as PM in 1990, shortly before the first Gulf War, which she had egged on – and in the face of serious opposition to her iniquitous poll tax. She lived to see Britain plunged into an economic crisis from which it still has not recovered, brought about in large part by her policies of deregulating the finance sector and fostering greed-driven capitalism. According to reports, she went slowly insane, afflicted with dementia for the last thirteen years of her life.

Perhaps Thatcher's most shameful legacy was facilitating the destruction of an alternative political voice representing the viewpoint of ordinary people. Her long-term political crony, Lord Howe of Aberavon[54] put it differently: *'Her real triumph was to have transformed not just one party but two, so that when Labour did eventually return, the great bulk of Thatcherism was accepted as irreversible.'* Indeed, the subsequent Labour Government under Tony Blah was 'labour' in nothing but name.

Whatever you may think of Hugo Chavez, he kept alive the belief in other possibilities - at considerable personal risk. He was actually ousted in 2002 by a coup (said by some to have been supported by the United States and the CIA). This belief is lent strength by the fact that the coup leaders had so little local support they were forced to hand back the reigns of power to Chavez after a mere forty-seven hours, making it possibly the shortest military takeover in history. Well, to be fair to Dame Margaret, she did survive an assassination attempt by the Irish Republican Army in 1984, and no one would deny that she had the courage of her dubious convictions. According to one source[55], she was turned down for a job in 1948 as a research chemist for ICI on the grounds that she was *'headstrong, obstinate and dangerously self-opinionated'*. Violence in Northern Ireland increased considerably in her first term of office, and nine IRA members died on hunger strikes in English prisons. After the assassination attempt, however, she did seem to moderate her stance on Ireland, so perhaps she was not entirely unresponsive to the alternative point-of-view.

---

54 http://www.margaretthatcher.org/document/110597

55 http://www.bbc.co.uk/news/uk-politics-10377842

Thatcher's economic policies have sometimes been credited with putting the 'Great' back in Great Britain – though the gloss seems to have gone off the 'Great'-ness again in the last year or two. Even at the time, however, it depended very much on where you were looking from. Her first term as Prime Minister saw a decline of thirty percent in manufacturing output, and unemployment reaching an all-time high of three million plus. Much of her apparent success could be attributed to the huge sell-off of state assets, and increased profits for the companies that survived.

After her resignation from active politics, Thatcher was employed by tobacco giant Philip Morris as a 'geopolitical consultant', in a role similar to that played by Aaron Eckhart in the 2005 movie *'Thank You For Smoking'* – only Thatcher was for real.

As for Hugo Chavez, it would be hard to find a national leader with more starkly contrasting economic and social policies. Undoubtedly, he had the major advantage of heading a country said to have the world's largest reserves of crude oil. Nevertheless, that doesn't seem necessarily to oblige a government to show concern for its people. Chavez's so-called 'Bolivarian Revolution' nationalised several key industries, increased spending on health and education, and aimed to develop systems facilitating participatory democracy. His 'Mission Zamora' was a reform programme aimed at redistributing land to the landless. Needless to say it was vehemently opposed by vested interests who hired assassins to terminate supporters and beneficiaries of the reforms. In 2009, Chavez and other like-minded South American leaders established the Bank of the South as an alternative to the International Monetary Fund, which they perceived as pursuing an unsympathetic political agenda. Former World Bank chief economist, Nobel Laureate and Columbia University professor Joseph Stiglitz is on record as expressing approval of this project.

Of course, Chavez had his critics abroad as well as at home. He did not endear himself to the Younger Bush's administration with his criticism of the US invasion of Iraq. The organisation *Human Rights Watch* issued a report in 2008 claiming that government action in Venezuela was eroding the independence of the judiciary and 'undercutting journalists' freedom of expression'. To put that in perspective, HRW's headquarters is in the

Empire State Building in New York City, and its principal source of funding is George Soros – of whom I have written before.

One example of the independence of the judiciary in Venezuela is a case involving a judge Maria Afiuni, who was arrested on charges of corruption. Apparently she had released on bail a banker charged with large-scale fraud and illegal currency trading. HRW and other groups including the US Department of State felt that the learned judge was being unfairly treated. Chavez's government was of the opinion that she might have been unduly influenced by under-the-table incentives. Who's to know?

Well, no doubt debate over the legacies of these two late lamented will go on, with little agreement possible between entrenched positions. Baroness Thatcher was seen off at a state funeral on Wednesday with much British pomp and ceremony. Sadly, some might feel, US President Obama was otherwise engaged, and Hilary Clinton apparently declined her invitation. In their stead the US was represented by George Schultz, Henry Kissinger and Dick Cheney – relics, one might think, of a more clearly defined political age. Former apartheid South African President FW de Clerk was there – but not Cristina Fernandez de Kirchner, current president of Argentina, who, I understand, was not invited.

Chavez's funeral was apparently a less formal, more musical affair. Ms de Kirchner was in attendance, as were Cuba's Raul Castro, Iran's Mahmoud Ahmedinejad, Bolivia's Evo Morales, and Belarus's Alexander Lukashenko as well as Brazil's Dilma Vana Rousseff. Actor Sean Penn and Hollywood director Oliver Stone had kind words to say, as did maverick film-maker Michael Moore, who quoted Chavez as saying, on their meeting in 2009, *'He was happy to finally meet someone Bush hated more than him.'* A man could have worse things inscribed on his tombstone.

26

Days of Rage - in Turkey

3 June 2013

I get angry sometimes. I try not to, but occasionally I can't help it. It's a natural human emotion. Mostly I get angry about things I can't control - which is stupid, I know, but again, I think, quite normal. I hate it when I see people in power abusing their positions of responsibility. I get angry when I see the powerful oppressing and exploiting the weak. I feel frustrated when I see weak people kowtowing to those in authority in order to advance their own careers.

Years ago in New Zealand I stood as a candidate for parliament. I tried to work through the system to bring about meaningful economic and social change for the benefit of the country. I saw close up the dirty tricks of the wealthy elite determined to hold on to power no matter the cost. I saw smear campaigns, electoral gerrymandering and control of the media. I saw the government of the day deliberately stir up an issue that polarised the nation and provoked violent street demonstrations leading to a crackdown by the forces of law and order. The result infuriated me. If I hadn't had a wife, three young children and a mortgage, I might have been tempted to violence myself. Gradually the fury gave way to sadness, and eventually to resignation.

Well, donkeys live a long time, as a former colleague used to observe (thanks Alan). On Sunday morning I took my bicycle over to Taksim, the main centre of Istanbul's entertainment industry, five-star hotels and foreign diplomats. My plan had been to take part in a ride across the Bosporus Bridge, organised by environmentalist groups. I knew it would be cancelled, but I went anyway. Partly I was psyched up for a good bike ride, and partly I was curious. I wanted to see for myself the situation in the square after the previous day's demonstrations.

Taksim Square and the surrounding streets looked a little like the pictures we saw from the recent tornado in Oklahoma: footpaths torn up, bricks and stones lying thick all around; makeshift barricades, shells of buses, overturned cars and minibuses, burnt out police vehicles, everywhere graffiti (much of it obscene), bottles, beer cans, vast quantities of rubbish, and one or two small bands of determined protesters – a few supporters of the Kurdish BDP, a larger group of Marxist Leninists around the flag-draped Statue of the Republic in the centre of the square, homeless sleeping off the excitement or sitting around fires still burning in the disputed park.

I saw a couple of young students picking up rubbish around the statue, and I joined them with plastic bags purchased from a nearby supermarket. In the store, my eyes and throat were burning from traces of the pepper spray or tear gas employed by police the night before. As I filled my bags with the detritus of democracy, I was approached by a young man who identified himself as a reporter from *'Foreign Policy'*. I guess he was happy to find someone he could interview in English. *'Do you think Turkey has become increasingly polarized?'* he asked. *'Do you think this event has united all the disparate opposition groups in Turkey?'* No, and no again - and I'll tell you why.

Since I came to Turkey, in fact, pretty much since the beginning of the Republic, Taksim Square has been off-limits for large political gatherings. Apparently there was a brief experiment in the mid-1970s. On 1 May 1977 there was a huge gathering known to history as the Taksim Square

Massacre. Forty people were killed and 120 badly injured. Some, including the Leader of the Opposition, Bülent Ecevit, claimed links to the undercover *Gladio* organisation[56]. Prime Minister at the time was Süleyman Demirel, later removed from office by the military takeover of 1980. He remained, or perhaps became, a staunch Kemalist and republican, returning to office in 1991, before resigning in 1993 in favour of his protégé, Turkey's first woman PM. In gratitude, Tansu Çiller had him appointed to the Presidency, a role he filled for the next seven years.

In 2009, Turkey's AK Party government made 1 May an official holiday. However, there was anger in some circles this year when they refused to allow a commemoration of the 1977 incident to be held in the square. Good call or bad? Who knows? A government may not feel that large political demonstrations under the noses of well-heeled foreign tourists are good for the country's image.

To be fair, the AKP government has achieved much since taking office in 2003. They curbed Turkey's banana republic hyperinflation and have presided over a period of unprecedented economic growth, evidenced by a rapid increase in the proportion of citizens in the middle classes. They have provided the longest period of political stability Turkey has seen since free elections began. They kept the country out of the Iraq invasion while staying friends with the USA, and more recently have applied some much-needed pressure to the Israeli government over its intransigent attitude to the Palestinian question. Internally, they have opened up discussions addressing the country's problems with its large Kurdish and Alevi minorities. They have maintained interest in European Union membership while making it clear that Turkey is not desperate to join. I could go on, but you get the picture.

Getting back to the build up of rage. Turkey's (Istanbul's) secular Kemalist elite has had things its own way pretty much since Day One of the modern Republic. Atatürk himself managed fifteen years as President without troubling himself to hold an election. His successor, Ismet İnönü

---

56 http://en.wikipedia.org/wiki/Operation_Gladio

held two – the first in 1946, more for show than anything else – the second, in 1950 leading to the election of a new governing party, the Democrats, and Turkey's first popularly elected Prime Minister, Adnan Menderes.

There was a bit of a roller-coaster ride in the country's politics for the next fifty years. Menderes himself was ousted by a military coup in 1960 and subsequently hanged along with two of his ministers. Elected governments were again removed by direct military intervention in 1970 and 1980; and once less violently when the generals had a quiet word in PM Necmettin Erbakan's ear in 1997, following which he quietly left of his own accord.

One of PM Erdoğan's more controversial achievements in his ten-year stewardship has been the trial in civilian courts of senior military personnel accused of plotting another coup to remove him – and overseeing amendments to the constitution allowing the courts to try officers involved in the brutal 1980 coup. Undoubtedly Tayyip Bey has made a few powerful enemies.

Again, from pretty much the first day of taking office, Erdoğan upset the secular Kemalists by appearing in public with his headscarved wife Emine Hanım. A good number of his ministers committed the same offence, arousing the fury of the Istanbul urban elite. To make matters worse, his government lifted the ban on the wearing of headscarves by female university students. Tayyip Erdoğan is a devout, practising Muslim – a fact which, in a country where ninety-nine percent of the population are of that faith, certainly helped him to become the first Turkish PM in living memory to lead a government with a parliamentary majority.

Ironically, their parliamentary ascendancy is perhaps one of AKP's major disadvantages. Turkey's biggest problem in the last ten years has been the lack of a credible parliamentary opposition. Underlining the dearth of ideas in the secular urban elite camp, the Republican People's Party (CHP) returned from the political wilderness in 1992 (whither it had been sent by the generals after the 1980 coup). With little going for them other than their claim to be the direct descendants of Atatürk's very own party, they became the second-largest group in parliament after the 2002 elections. Since then they have distinguished themselves by saying 'NO' to pretty much everything proposed by the government, and doing their best to stir up popular unrest, while, at the same time, failing to come up with a single positive idea of their own.

Predictably, this seems to have led to a growing arrogance by the Prime Minister and his party. As English politician and historian Lord Acton famously said, *'Power tends to corrupt, and absolute power corrupts absolutely.'* No doubt this arrogance has been encouraged by the fact that Turks actually like (and perhaps need) a strongman. Nevertheless, the number of Turks getting p---d off with the government has undoubtedly been increased by a feeling that self-righteous religiosity has begun to replace reasoned public debate.

Who would ever have thought that Turks could be stopped from smoking a cigarette whenever and wherever they chose? Now smokers are under threat of extinction and, even as a non-smoker, I am starting to feel sympathy for them. While I agree that smokers, alcohol-drinkers and drivers of huge SUVs should contribute to the environmental and health costs associated with their addictions, it does seem unfair that Turks, with an average income at the lower end of the OECD spectrum, should have to pay the highest petrol prices in the world. A little study of US history would show that banning alcohol will inevitably have undesirable social consequences – and driving prices sky-high with exorbitant taxation will stimulate a black-market whose main beneficiaries will be organized crime syndicates and political dissidents.

Personally I have no problem with the building of two or three symbolic mosques in high profile locations on the Asian side of Istanbul – but I'm not happy to be woken every morning before sunrise by five minutes or more of highly amplified Arabic chant summoning to prayer a public, large numbers of whom intend exercising their democratic right not to go.

However, I apologise for straying from the main point of this post, which was, I admit, to address the matter of the protests in Istanbul's Taksim Square and in dozens of other cities around Atatürk's Republic. Ostensibly, the protests were triggered by the plan to rebuild an Ottoman military barracks on a not-very-large park adjacent to the iconic meeting place. Now if you know Istanbul you will be aware that Taksim Square is a singularly stark and barren concrete space whose most interesting feature is a large sculpture representing Mustafa Kemal Atatürk himself. On one side is the 1960s soviet-style Atatürk Culture Centre, adjacent to another relic of the tasteless 60s, a twenty-storey hotel from the glass-box school of architecture, thankfully known as the Marmara. Opposite the culture centre is a windowless brick structure that I think is a reservoir, and on the fourth side a kind of bus terminal behind which, and largely invisible unless you are in it, a small park generally occupied by homeless individuals and itinerant alcoholics. In the middle of the square is a large island where you can access a major line of the city's underground Metro system – if you can reach it, given that the island is isolated by a circular speedway around which hurtles an unbroken torrent of buses, yellow taxis, minibuses and private cars.

As far as I can understand it, the plan was to divert traffic underground and turn the whole area into a vehicle-free zone which would then be landscaped. The bus terminal and little-used park area would be redeveloped by building a replica of the architecturally striking 19th century artillery barracks demolished in 1940. The intention was to utilize the rebuilt structure as hotel accommodation, shopping, a museum, cultural centre, whatever. Not such a bad thing, you might think.

The problem seems to be that the cutting of trees in the park became a focus for the pent-up rage that has clearly been building up in Istanbul and other Turkish cities for several years. To return to the questions posed by Justin, the reporter from 'Foreign Policy': 'Has Turkish society become polarised in recent years? And has this event united the political opposition?' In the sense that opposition to the present government has brought together a host of unlikely bed-mates, from residents of Istanbul's plushest districts to the most radical of communist ideologues, yes. But if you are asking whether this 'unity' will translate into anything resembling a credible political party with a serious alternative political agenda, I fear not. As the 16th century Protestant reformer, Martin Luther said, 'The mad mob does *not ask how it could be better, only that it be different. And when it then becomes worse, it must change again. Thus they get bees for flies, and at last hornets for bees.'*

Nevertheless, citizens of Turkey have ample grounds for dissatisfaction. Workplace rights, conditions, wages and salaries are substandard, especially in the private sector where collective bargaining is a no-no. The education system is in a sad state with little chance of fulfilling Atatürk's dream of producing a modern educated populace. There is an appalling gulf between the extremes of rich and poor. I am currently reading *'The Histories'* of Herodotus, and I came across a delightful solution for this last problem: The Egyptian Pharaoh *'Amasis,'* he says, *'established an admirable custom which Solon borrowed and introduced at Athens . . . this was that every man once a year should declare before the provincial governor, the source of his livelihood; failure to do this, or inability to prove that the source was an honest one, was punishable by death.'*

On the other hand, conditions for the majority in Turkey have improved out of sight since I first came to the country. What worries me now, in fact *scares* me would be a better word, is that the country may descend into a chaos from which only another period of martial law will save it. Sadly, I also fear that there are forces outside of Turkey who would welcome that, and have been working behind the scenes to make it happen.

27

Rebetika and Zorba the Turk

18 June 2013

'Those who cannot remember the past are condemned to repeat it.' These, I now know, were the actual words (frequently misquoted) of the Spanish-American writer George Santayana. Well, quote or misquote, the message is clear. Sadly, I see this failure of memory all around me. I read an interview the other day with a Turkish artist who, talking of recent political demonstrations in Istanbul and elsewhere, claimed that respect for human rights, women's rights, freedom of expression and freedom of speech had declined in this country in the past ten years. As a close observer of events over the past eighteen years, I was surprised. If he had kept to the issue of the preservation of a green area in Taksim, I could have understood his anger - but to make that claim in a country with such a recent history of military coups, civilian disappearances, torture, suppression of minorities, honour killings, and corruption in government, civil service and football is beyond laughable.

Still, there it is. The guy said it, the female interviewer recorded it, the Western media published it, and their public, for lack of an alternative point of view, or perhaps just because they want to, probably believe it. What is sadder, however, is I imagine that guy, as an artist, had a fairly good education, and a lot of other educated young people in Turkey also seem to believe it.

Well, I have written my last words about the Taksim protests. What I want to talk about here is music, and its power to bring people together, if only we can hear its message. I want to talk about a musical genre whose history and origins, even in its homeland(s), are little known or else misunderstood. The reason, in fact, is not solely attributable to the ignorance of the local people. Rather, it is that the history of these people, over the past two centuries, has been so full of trauma and upheaval that they have willingly chosen to forget, and their governments have actually encouraged this process of forgetting, in the interests of building new nations from the ashes of old. So, first of all, a little historical background.

The 1964 Hollywood movie *'Zorba the Greek'* helped to popularise, at home and abroad, a genre of folk music and dance accompanied by a stringed instrument commonly known as bouzouki. Well, Hollywood is Hollywood, of course – and in our heart of hearts we know we shouldn't accept as gospel all we see on the silver screen. Nevertheless, in the absence of personal knowledge or experience, we may unintentionally incorporate the celluloid tale into our world-view.

A theme I find myself often returning to is the question of how to define a Turk. I have dealt at some length with the complex fabric of history in this part of the world, into which the Turkish invaders wove themselves after their arrival in the 11th century. I have touched on the intermarriage and intermingling of the Ottoman elite with their Christian and Jewish fellow citizens over the course of their six hundred-year empire. I have discussed the huge influx of refugees from the Crimea, the Caucasus, the Greek peninsula and the Balkans over a two hundred and fifty year period as neighbouring states gained independence from and/or expanded into Ottoman territory, displacing as they did so, their Muslim neighbours who had lived there for centuries.

Parallel to this theme, I have found myself criticising the modern state of Greece, and its Western supporters for what sometimes seems a deliberate distortion of history. Part of the problem, as I have been at pains to explain, stems from the use in English of one word, 'Greek' to refer to three quite distinct historical and even geographical entities: first, the Ancient Greece of Homer, Socrates, Herodotus and Pythagoras; second, the medieval Byzantine Eastern Roman-Greek Empire; and finally, the modern Kingdom/Republic founded, with the help of Great Britain, France and Russia, in 1830.

Our lack of satisfactory English words to distinguish these three entities, coupled with a sometimes deliberate blurring of the distinctions for political purposes, has made for serious misunderstandings that continue to bedevil international affairs, as, for example, in the case of the Cyprus issue. What I overlooked, however, in my sympathy for the plight of the Republic of Turkey, was the fact that, quite understandably, the government and citizens of modern Greece also experience ongoing problems of identity as a direct result of their traumatic history.

I read recently a book entitled *'Greece, the Hidden Centuries*[57] which described the period from the fall of Constantinople in 1453 to the establishment of the Kingdom of Greece in 1830 – a period of nearly four centuries when Christian, Muslim and Jew lived together in an Empire that did not suppress religious, linguistic or cultural identity. In reality, the period of cohabitation extends several centuries before the final conquest of the Byzantine Greek capital. The implications of that time span make nonsense of most attempts to separate 'Greek' and 'Turkish' cultures.

Another theme running through these posts is the idea that the same historical event may be remembered, described and interpreted in different ways depending on how it impacted on those involved. I have written elsewhere of my surprise at learning that Turks celebrate 18 March as their victory day in the campaign we refer to as Gallipoli, when New Zealanders and Australians remember 25 April as the day we (Anzacs) arrived on the scene.

---

57 *Greece, the Hidden Centuries*, David Brewer, (IB Tauris, 2012)

Turks and Greeks have a similar problem with the event known to historians variously as the Liberation War, the Turkish War of Independence, the Greco-Turkish War or the Asia Minor Catastrophe. For citizens of Turkey, victory in that three-year war opened the door for the establishment of an independent republic. For Greeks, on the other hand, defeat meant the bitter end of their Great Dream - the reincarnation of the once mighty Eastern Orthodox Christian Byzantine Empire centred on the legendary city of Constantinople.

But that's not all. Military retreat from Asia Minor in 1922 was a huge reality check for the Greeks who had begun their campaign with encouragement from the European powers victorious in the First World War. Subsequently, seeing the writing of Turkish nationalist victory on the wall, Britain, France and the others abandoned the Greek cause and left their little neo-classical cousins to their fate. That fate they still remember as the Asia Minor Disaster, when up to 1.5 million people identified as Christians were uprooted from their ancestral homes and shipped across the sea to be resettled in mainland Greece. Who were these people?

Sea-faring tribes speaking a language we think of as Ancient Greek spread around the Aegean and Black Seas from the early centuries of the First Millennium BCE, settling on the islands and the mainland coasts. Sometimes conquering and sometimes forming neighbourly relations with the local peoples, they developed cultures classicists know as Hellenic, Aeolian, Ionian and Dorian, which non-academics tend to unite under the blanket term 'Greek'. This culture is characterised by distinctive features of literature, architecture, sculpture, food and music which, of necessity, incorporated earlier local elements.

Their literature tells us of struggles against their powerful neighbours, the Persians, and the triumphs of the Great Hellenic hero, Alexander, in the pre-Christian millennium. Less well-publicised was their forced incorporation into the classical Roman Empire in 146 BCE. Their history re-emerges somewhat murkily into European consciousness after the adoption of Christianity as that empire's state religion, and the subsequent fall of the city of Rome, leaving Constantinople as capital of a now Christian, largely Greek-speaking Eastern Roman Empire.

It also brings us, after a lengthy but necessary introduction, to real subject of this post: the musical genre known as *rebetika*. When the Greek army entered Anatolia in May 1919, they were welcomed as liberators by the predominantly Greek Orthodox Christian inhabitants. When, three years later, the Turkish nationalist forces drove out the invading army, the position of those Christian citizens of the Ottoman Empire, now perceived as traitors, was clearly untenable. I have not the time or space here to examine the claims and counter claims of property destruction and human atrocities that took place in these years. Suffice it to say that an exchange of populations took place, whereby Christians from Anatolia (Asia Minor) went to mainland Greece, and vice versa Muslims from the other side of the Aegean.

Those Christians, numbering, it is generally agreed, around 1.5 million, arrived in a poor country with a total population of around seven million. Many of them were educated middle class people with a good standard of living who now found themselves homeless, jobless and destitute. They brought with them little besides the cultural identity forged by twenty-five centuries in Asia, the last six of them, side by side with Muslims of Turkish ancestry.

The musical genre that flourished in the sub-culture inhabited by these 'Asiatic' Greeks is known as *rebetika*, and attained its peak of artistic expression in the 1930s. It has been called the 'Greek Blues' – not because of any similarity of sound, but because it was the musical expression of the soul of a dispossessed people. Performers and audiences were alienated from mainstream society by their poverty and foreign identity, their association with crime and prisons, with drug use and alcohol, and with disreputable bars and cafes.

The very word *rebetika* is problematic, and has spawned its own academic field of study, *rebetology*. One problem for the layperson is the alternative form *rembetika*. This has come about in typical English fashion, whereby scholars or other intellectuals employ peculiar features of spelling in an attempt to represent the etymology of a word. Words of Greek origin suffer particularly from this affectation, as in the use of the letter 'c' to represent the Greek letter *kappa*, and 'ph' to represent Φ (F). The Greek letter that looks like a B is actually pronounced as V. The B sound is represented in Greek by the digraph 'MP'. Well, scholars love to show off their knowledge, so in goes the M to the English word. Unfortunately, P is P in both languages, so with a patronising nod to actual pronunciation, B was substituted. Stick with *rebetika*, and you'll be fine.

Then there is the Greek-ness of the music, which, according to Hollywood's *Zorba*, is essential and fundamental. However, in the light of the history outlined above, we will be not at all surprised to find the same songs being sung on the eastern coast of the Aegean, and clearly not because they were imported from Greece. Again, unsurprisingly, Zorba's famous dance and some key vocabulary associated with *Rebetika* music, reflect the genre's Anatolian origins - though the use of Greek or English versions of Ottoman place names in the literature tends to mask this. The folk dance known as *hasapiko* is said to have originated in Constantinople (Istanbul); *zeybekiko* and *tsifteteli* are clearly derived from Turkish words. The *zeybeks* were irregular militia of nomadic *yörük* origins with a kind of Robin Hood reputation for protecting poor villagers from rapacious landlords. Their characteristic male dance is well known in Turkey, as is the *çiftetelli*, a chain of dancers, often performed at weddings and other social celebrations.

One source I read claimed that the bouzouki was unknown in Asia Minor - but a more credible writer gave the origin of the word as the Turkish *bozuk*, which was apparently applied to a kind of tuning. Certainly the *bağlama* is everywhere seen and heard in Turkey, and its origin has been traced to ancient Mesopotamia. A feature of *Rebetika* is the *taksim*, a kind of improvised solo often introducing the song and setting the mood, as well as demonstrating the virtuosity of the musician. That source above stated that the word comes from Arabic, which it may well do - but it is nevertheless used in Turkish, and undoubtedly came to Greece with those Anatolian refugees.

Well, this is not a competition. It doesn't really matter whether you call those small cups of strong coffee with the annoying centimetre of sediment, Turkish or Greek. *Gyros* or *döner kebap*, they both taste good in a sandwich. The simple fact is that people who live as neighbours and intermarry for centuries will inevitably share aspects of their separate cultures, taking and giving until whose is what and what is whose will be lost in the mists of time.

Unfortunately for the majority who just want to live their lives, raise their children and wash down their *gyros* with a Turkish coffee, history, like religion, can become a political football. Politicians and other seekers after power love using *'-isms'* to divide and rule, to unite their supporters and manufacture an enemy.

The concept of nationalism that blossomed in Europe from the romantic movement of the late 18th century began as a search for cultural roots lost in the modernisation and urbanisation of the agrarian and industrial revolutions. It was quickly seized on, however, by political leaders, to unite and divide. The Ottoman Empire, consisting as it did, of diverse religious and cultural groups, and occupying territory coveted by rival empires, was particularly vulnerable.

It's painful to lose an empire. Ask the Brits. When you've once ruled extensive dominions on which the sun never set, it's not easy to adjust to being the world's sixth largest economy and a relatively minor player on the stage of international affairs. You can't help hoping the good times will come again. For the Greeks, the loss of their imperial capital Constantinople and their subservience to the Ottomans were wounds that never healed. As Ottoman power declined and powerful 'friends' in Europe encouraged them to imagine that their former lands could be recovered, it was all too easy to believe.

The 'Asia Minor Disaster' was brought about by the manipulation of European powers for their own political and economic ends. Greeks were encouraged in a highly questionable enterprise, and left in the lurch when the project went sour. Sadly, albeit understandably, the Greeks subsequently focused their anger and frustration on their Turkish neighbours rather than on the foreign powers who should by rights shoulder the blame. If you want to read more about *rebetika* music, I can recommend two articles, *Rebetika: An Historical Introduction*[58] and *Rebetika, A Brief History*[59]. They do, however, contain certain statements that contribute to misunderstanding about the historical background. Muslims were expelled from Greece, the first writer says, *'mainly because the Greek government needed land and homes in which to settle the refugees'*, suggesting that the process was begun by the Turks. The second writer goes a stage further. *'Greek-speaking Turks from the present entity of Greece were shipped en masse to Turkey, and Greeks from what is now Turkey were shipped to Greece (many of them in the face of murder, rape and torture at the hands of the Turks, intent on repeating their massacre of the Armenians).'* The Greeks, we are to understand, were innocent angels in the business. Are we also to assume that the atrocities they committed against each other in their own civil war of the late 1940s they had learnt from Turks?

History and music have lessons to teach us, if we approach both with an open mind. Name-calling and finger-pointing, on the other hand, produce little but misunderstanding and hatred. Listen to the sad voices of *rebetika*. Try to bridge the gulf and heal the wounds.

---

58 http://mediterraneanpalimpsest.wordpress.com/2013/01/24/an-historical-introduction-to-rebetika/

59 http://www.rebetology.com/hydragathering/2002emery-history.html

28

On Artifact Smuggling, Religious Tolerance and the Winter Olympics

25 July 2013

History, as I have remarked before, is a fascinating subject, rather less certain in its account of events than ordinary citizens may be generally aware. One of the reasons for starting this blog was my discovery, after coming to live in Turkey, that the version of affairs in this part of the world that I had grown up with did not always accord with the way people around here viewed them.

Another example of this came to my attention as I made my annual trip to the Aegean town of Selçuk to visit two English friends. Selçuk has long been a popular base for tourists visiting the sites of cities and temples important in the ancient classical world: Ephesus, Miletos, Didyma, Priene and more. Recently it seems to have become increasingly popular with Christians flocking to see the actual locations of events seminal to the establishment of their own religion.

In spite of their reputation in the Western world, Muslims have never had major objections to Christians practising that religion. Arabs and Turks may have conquered and occupied the 'Holy Lands' for around 1,200 years, but they were fairly tolerant of pilgrims from Christendom wishing to visit. Unlike their Christian contemporaries, who couldn't even get on with each other, Ottoman Sultans ruled a vast Empire that included all shades of Muslims and Christians, and offered sanctuary to Jews fleeing persecution by European overlords.

All the guidebooks will tell you that the population of modern Turkey is ninety-nine percent Muslim – yet ironically many locations mentioned in the Bible's Old and New Testaments lie within its borders. Especially targeted by Catholic tourists is the house said to have been the residence of Mary, the mother of Jesus, who is believed to have come to the city of Ephesus after her son's crucifixion. On the citadel hill of Selçuk itself are the remains of a huge basilica church, erected by the Roman/Byzantine/ Greek Emperor Justinian in the 6th century over a grave supposed to be last resting place of Jesus's favourite disciple John.

It is a credit to the people and government of Turkey that, not only do they respect these sites of enormous significance to Christian history, but they also allow foreign Christian organisations to restore and maintain them, and even display their own descriptions and commentaries. A text to be seen at the entrance to the basilica site is credited to the *American Society of Ephesus*, whose HQ, apparently, is in Lima, Ohio. The text provides details of the life of John, with Biblical references, and the history of the church itself. One sentence in particular caught my eye because some words had been scratched out. *'Prior ~~to the invasion~~ by the Seldjuk Turks, the town of Selcuk was known as Ayasoluk, meaning 'Devine* [sic] *Theologian' in honor of St John.'* Leaving aside the minor errors in the sentence, the interesting thing for me was that beneath the scratched-out section was the hand-written, barely legible word *'conquest'*. It may be a small amendment, but is nonetheless indicative of a slightly different take on the history of Asia Minor – a part of the world that has had countless conquerors over many millennia.

Well, one consequence of that Turkish invasion, or conquest, was perhaps that less value was given to the temples, churches and artwork of their predecessors, the Greeks, Romans, and Byzantines. There's nothing unusual in that, of course. When the Roman Empire turned to Christianity, pagan temples were destroyed, mined for their stonework, or converted to new uses such as churches. Statues celebrating the naked human body had breasts and genitalia chiselled off. Interest in Classical civilisations and their artifacts is a relatively recent development in Western Europe, accelerating from the later years of the 18th century.

One result was a rising popularity in exploring the cities and temples of antiquity, and whisking away statuary and other relics to private collections. The building of public museums really began with the British Museum in 1759, and blossomed into the 'Museum Age' in the USA in the late 19th and early 20th centuries. Consequently, in the 19th century the removal of ancient treasures became more organised, professional, and at least more for the benefit of a wider public. There is much debate these days on the subject of archaeological finds displayed in museums around the world. However, it was only in the early years of the 20th century that stricter controls were placed on the removal of ancient artifacts, so it is difficult to make a strong case for the return of pieces taken prior to that. Nevertheless, there is an argument that major relics such as the so-called *Elgin Marbles* would be better displayed in Athens than their present location in London WC1.

During my brief stay in the town of Selçuk, I visited again the remains of the ancient city Magnesia-on-Meander. I was fortunate to have two knowledgeable guides in my friends Robert and Adrian, without whom much of the richness of the city would have remained unknown to me. The site is located some 30 kilometres south of the better-known city of Ephesus and the two seem to have been of a similar size, which makes Magnesia very attractive to archaeologists.

The first of these to begin serious exploration was a French team around 1840. They were particularly interested in a large temple dedicated to the goddess Artemis, a major deity in this part of the world, and worshipped in Magnesia as *Artemis Leukophryene*, she of the white eyebrows. It was said that the goddess had appeared to the inhabitants of the city prior to construction of the temple, and the building was ingeniously designed so that, at certain times of the year, the light of a full moon would shine through an opening above the main entrance, progressively illuminating the statue of Artemis inside, recreating the epiphany to the wonderment of assembled worshippers.

The Magnesia Artemesion may not have been as grand as its counterpart in Ephesus, renowned as one of the Wonders of the Ancient World – but still it was one of the larger Hellenistic temples, built around 200 BCE, architecturally innovative and boasting a 175 metre-long frieze depicting the mythological war between the Greeks and the Amazons. A forty-metre section of the magnificent frieze subsequently found its way to the Louvre Museum in Paris where it may still be seen. A further twenty metres, along with many other finds were later relocated to the Pergamon Museum in Berlin after a German team of archaeologists carried out excavations in the 1890s.

Since 1984, archaeologists from Ankara University have been working at the Magnesia site. With Turkish nationals overseeing the dig, and international agreements in place to outlaw the smuggling of antiquities, you might think that the treasures of Turkey would be safe at last – but you would be wrong. In 1989 excavations began uncovering a building identified as the Market Basilica, and the most remarkable find was an elaborately carved column capital featuring a scene from the 'Odyssey' of Homer in which two fearsome monsters, Charybdis and Scylla, combined forces to devour Odysseus's crew of sailors. When discovered, the capital was in near-perfect condition, but almost immediately persons unknown, unable to make off with the entire 3.5 tonne marble block, contrived to break off the head and right arm of the monster Scylla which, we must assume, found their way to some private collection abroad.

A more famous case involves the unearthing of a stash of treasure known as the Lydian or Croesan Hoard. Croesus, proverbially one of the richest rulers in the ancient world, was king of the Kingdom of Lydia in the 6th century BCE, with his capital at Sardis in Western Turkey. The site was illegally excavated in the 1960s, a small hoard of buried treasure found, and the loot sold off, again, to persons unknown. Eventually some of the items turned up at an exhibition in the New York Metropolitan

Museum of Art, resulting in an expensive six-year legal battle initiated by the Turkish Government.

After the court case, the artifacts were returned to Turkey where they went on display in the Uşak Archaeological Museum, but in 2006 it was discovered, due to an anonymous tip-off, that some of the pieces were fake. An investigation revealed that a gang which included the Director of the Museum had been selling them off and substituting imitations in their place. Following negotiations with officials of a museum in Germany, a golden brooch in the shape of a winged seahorse, identified as part of the missing hoard, was returned to Turkey.

Just this week, another similar theft came to light. In 2000, excavations at the site of the ancient city of Akmonya, also in the Uşak Province, brought to light a floor mosaic from the classical Roman period depicting the goddess Tyche/Fortuna. Shortly after being unearthed, the mosaic, measuring 75 cm by 150 cm, was stolen from the site. As a result of investigations by Interpol and a special branch of the Turkish Police with responsibilities for artifact smuggling, a gang of eight persons was apprehended with the mosaic in their possession. After thirteen years they were in the process of spiriting the goddess out of the country – an indication of how valuable the trade is, how organised the criminals are, and how difficult it is to catch them.

To conclude this discussion, and to illustrate the extent to which millennia of civilisations overlap in this remarkable country, as well as to indicate how that history continues to influence, for better or worse, events of the present, I would like to take you back to the site of ancient Magnesia-on-Meander. Not far from the Artemesion temple is the shell of a medium-sized mosque dating from the Beylik period in the early 15th century – a kind of intervening age of smaller fiefdoms or principalities following the collapse of the Seljuk Turkish Empire, and before the rise of the Ottomans. Interestingly, however, the mosque is known by the name of *Çerkez Musa*, or Moses the Circassian. Apparently a group of refugees from the Caucasus area established a village here in the 18th century after fleeing from Russian imperial expansion – the beginnings of a programme of Russification and ethnic cleansing of Muslims that continued for two centuries and is still causing problems today.

One of these problems is centred on the city preparing to host the 2014 Winter Olympics. Sochi lies in the eastern Black Sea region beside the Caucasus Mountains, and word has it that it will host the most expensive games ever, winter or summer! The estimated price tag of $50 billion is said to have been substantially inflated by extensive bribery and corruption. Who can know? But one thing seems certain: the local and international Circassian community will be using the occasion to publicise their claims of atrocities, expulsion and genocide that allegedly took place after the Russian military machine completed its conquest of the territory in 1864. I guess we can be equally confident that the Russian state will be doing its best to ensure that high volume celebrations of Olympic competition and togetherness drown out whatever message the Circassians try to convey to the outside world.

Which brings me back to our starting point – my constant rediscovering, in this quarter of the planet, that many of the historical *'facts'* I thought I knew, turn out, at the very least, to be highly debatable. There are two sides to almost every story, and in the interests of fair play, we should maintain an open mind to the possibility of alternative versions.

29

Piyale Pasha - the man and the mosque

26 August 2013

Istanbul is a huge city. Visitors from abroad tend to concentrate on the Sultanahmet (Blue Mosque) area of the old city, and the shopping/entertainment neighbourhood of Taksim/Beyoğlu. The modern expansion of the city began in the late 1960s when the population was around two million. Now the official count is 13.5 million, but, as with other cities in the megalopolis class, a lot depends on where you draw the boundaries.

In the 16th century, at the peak of Ottoman power, the imperial capital of Istanbul/Constantinople was still enclosed within the twenty-two kilometres of defensive walls built by the Roman emperor Theodosius II in the 5th century. Nevertheless there was, in addition, much activity outside. The satellite settlement of Galata across the Golden Horn continued its role as trading centre and residential suburb for non-citizens of the empire: Venetians, Genoese and other Europeans drawn by the magnetic attraction of this gateway to the East. The town of Scutari/Üsküdar on the Asian shore served as launching pad for the pageantry and adventure of annual pilgrimages to the Muslims' holy city of Mecca. The Ottoman navy, scourge of the Mediterranean littoral, had its main base, shipyards, cannon foundries and other associated industries on the northern shore of the Golden Horn and around the corner as far as the Bosporus village of Beşiktaş.

Despite the exponential growth of Istanbul's population, and fears, or at least claims, that the present government of Turkey has been trying to recreate a neo-Ottoman sphere of influence, those glory days of empire are long gone. Passenger ferries and other small craft were still being built in the Golden Horn shipyards in the 1980s, and repairs carried out in the dry-dock until more recently - but the decision has at last been taken, as in London and other world cities, to find new uses for the disused dock-lands area: a hotel or two, modern shopping no doubt, recreational facilities such as parks and cycleways. You can observe the pattern in Liverpool, Gloucester, Melbourne, Australia, even my own hometown of Auckland, New Zealand.

Of course those docklands areas contain much of their cities' heritage, and sensitive redevelopment must include preservation of buildings with historical significance, perhaps adapting them for modern purposes such as up-market apartments, museums and art galleries. One advantage of such urban renewal is that it brings new life and visitors to parts of a city that may have been neglected no-go zones for many years.

One such area of Istanbul is the neighbourhood of Kasımpaşa. The current Prime Minister of Turkey, Tayyip Erdoğan, continues to attract more than his fair share of criticism, and one sticking point for some modern Turks seems to be that he was born and raised in this 'mahalle' which, if there were a railway track nearby, would definitely be on the 'wrong' side. For his part, the PM seems quite proud of his humble origins – and they may arguably contribute to his popularity among the less exalted echelons of Turkish society.

On Sunday I ventured, in the company of a Turkish friend, into the interior of the 'hood in search of a mosque I had seen from a distance, but never visited. Perhaps it's a measure of the status of Kasımpaşa that the taxi driver we hailed to drive us had no idea about the location or even the existence of Piyale Pasha Mosque, and dropped us off within sight of another one nearer the waterfront – or perhaps, on reflection, he was nervous about plunging too far into unknown territory.

By dint of asking directions and walking a kilometre or so, we did eventually arrive at the building we were seeking – a large 16th century stone edifice set in an uncharacteristically (for Istanbul) green area of fig trees, walnuts and market gardens. There is some mystery about the building itself, in part because its design is also uncharacteristic of mosques of the Ottoman Imperial period. The general rule, modelled on the great cathedral of Hagia Sophia, is a large single dome covering the inner sanctuary – but Piyale Pasha, or his architect perhaps, reverted to an earlier design with six smaller domes supported by two granite columns in the prayer area. Most sources credit the mosque to the architect Sinan, shining star of Ottoman architecture – but the unusual design leaves some room for doubt.

Piyale Pasha himself seems to have been an interesting character, not least because he chose to locate his memorial mosque far from the capital's commercial and residential hub. Sources say he was of Croatian origin, captured (in battle?) and brought at the age of eleven to Istanbul where he was then educated in the palace itself. He went on to become a provincial governor and later an admiral in the imperial navy, testimony to the eclectic and meritocratic nature of Ottoman society at the time.

Surprisingly, Piyale Pasha is not well known, even in Turkey, despite marrying the daughter of Sultan Selim II and becoming his grand vizier. His fame is overshadowed by older colleagues, Barbaros Hayrettin Pasha and Turgut Reis. Nevertheless, he seems to have achieved considerable success in his own right, his raids on coastal towns of Italy and Spain forcing Christian states into some semblance of unity to defend their territories. Ottoman forces in the second half of the 16th century came to control the Aegean and much of the Mediterranean, including the North African coast and the strategic island of Cyprus – which, incidentally, they seized from the Venetians, not the Greeks.

Perhaps Admiral Piyale suffers from his close association with a sultan often considered to have begun his empire's downward slide. Certainly Selim II had a hard act to follow. His father, Suleiman, known in English as *The Magnificent*, ruled for forty-five years, and is generally regarded as having presided over the Ottoman Golden Age. During his son's eight-year reign, on the other hand, Ottoman forces suffered major setbacks against Russia, and Christian Europe at the Battle of Lepanto. Selim apparently had a reputation for enjoying a tipple, and one of his achievements was reopening bars and *meyhanes* closed by his father in the later years of his rule. The *Wikipedia* entry asserts that the unlucky sultan died as a result of a head injury sustained when he fell in his bathroom after a session of over-indulgence.

Well, maybe that's one reason why PM Erdoğan has some reservations about the benefits of drinking alcohol. Certainly, when he breaks a bottle of sparkling grape juice over the third Bosporus Bridge in the opening ceremony, he will want to make it clear that the structure will be named for Sultan Selim I and not Selim II.

In a more serious vein, I noticed, when visiting Admiral Piyale's mosque, recently renovated, that the *mihrab* (sacred altar) is beautifully decorated with ceramic tiles, and high on the walls runs a lengthy Koranic text in elegant Ottoman/Arabic calligraphy – while the rest of the walls and interior of the domes are uncharacteristically plain. Several articles I read stated that interior decoration had originally been more elaborate. They also noted that the mosque had been extensively rebuilt in the 19th century. Reading between the lines, it would seem that there was a time when Piyale Pasha Mosque fell into disuse and disrepair, and perhaps prey to theft and desecration.

Interestingly, Turkey's Ministry of Culture has begun taking steps to repatriate a display of tiles in the Paris Louvre Museum it claims were removed from the Kasımpaşa mosque and exported illegally. Authorities at the Louvre, needless to say, deny the claim, and say the tiles were acquired between 1871 and 1940 *'in conditions that were perfectly legal and in line with the rules of the time.'*

The *Wikipedia* entry says that *'a number of identical Iznik tiled lunette panels that are now on display in different museums including the Musée du Louvre in Paris, the Museu Calouste Gulbenkian in Lisbon and the Victoria and Albert Museum in London are believed to have been removed from the Piyale Pasha Mosque in the 19th century.'* It goes on to say that *'Two tiles from another lunette panel and a pair of tiles that probably came from the mihrab were sold at auction by Christie's in 2004.*

In fact, while roaming around the internet on this subject, I came across this item up for auction at Bonhams[60]: *'An Iznik pottery tile, Turkey, circa 1575, Provenance: Greek private collection: This elegant tile relates directly to lunette panels in the Louvre, the Musee des Art Decoratifs and the Gulbenkian Foundation. The first of these panels came from the Piyale Pasha Mosque (1573) in Istanbul.'*

Well, it's none of my business. I'm happy that Parisians and other visitors to the Louvre have the opportunity to see such examples of high Ottoman art – and if it helps them to a better understanding of their Muslim neighbours, perhaps the tiles should stay where they are.

---

60 http://www.bonhams.com/auctions/20833/lot/74/

30

Alevis in Turkey -
Is reconciliation possible?

9 September 2013

The English word *Turkey* (with a capital 'T') comes from the Turkish word *'Türkiye'* which means land of the Turks. It was not used by the Ottomans to describe their empire - but by Europeans to identify the Ottomans as 'other', to demonise, perhaps, and belittle a feared foe. The term really had no validity until 1923 when an indigenous army defeated an invading force from the Greek mainland, liberating the Anatolian heartland and the imperial capital Istanbul from foreign occupation.

The victorious leader, Mustafa Kemal Pasha (later Atatürk) and his team set about creating a new nation state from the ashes of the defunct Ottoman Empire. Without repeating details covered elsewhere, it is important to understand that the dissolution of that empire had been assisted by military defeats at the hands of foreign neighbours and nationalist liberation movements from within over the previous two centuries or more.

Building a new nation state required a philosophy and identity that citizens could relate to and fight for - the result was Turkish nationalism and the Republic of Turkey, not necessarily in that order. The pillars of that national identity were the Muslim religion, the Turkish language and

Turkish ethnicity, meaning a connection to the tribes that had poured out of Central Asia for centuries before the Ottomans hammered the last nail into the Byzantine Graeco-Roman coffin by conquering Constantinople in 1453.

The Muslim character of the new state was confirmed by an obligatory population exchange at the conclusion of the Independence War in 1923. Orthodox Christians, who were believed to have supported the Greek invasion, were dispatched to the Greek mainland, their places taken by Muslims sent in the opposite direction. Armenian Christians had already mostly been seen off in events I have also discussed elsewhere. Right from the very beginning, then, there was an uncomfortable disjunction inherent in the establishment of the new state: secularism was one of Atatürk's six founding principles, yet religion was a major determinant in the composition of Turkey's population.

Turkey is not alone in its discomfort, of course. The partition of British India after independence was won in 1947 involved a vast movement of population whereby Hindus from the newly created Pakistan were exchanged for Muslims from the new Union of India. Religion, language and ethnic origin may be powerful forces to be harnessed by ambitious political leaders seeking to foster unity and create a national identity. The melting pot of history, however, has produced a mix of humanity in which purity in any of those factors is, at best, elusive – and so it is in the Republic of Turkey, despite the best efforts of Kemalist lawmakers to legislate for 'Turkishness'.

In spite of the post-independence population exchange, modern India has almost as many followers of Islam as does Pakistan. Only one other country, Indonesia, has more Muslims. Similarly, many Eastern Orthodox and Armenian Christians continued to live in Turkey, especially Istanbul, though admittedly numbers declined as a result of international incidents, particularly involving next-door-neighbour, Greece. Members of the Jewish community have long made their homes in this part of the world, their numbers increased by refugees from the Spanish Inquisition in the 15th century. The republican state continued to grant them freedom of religion, language, education, culture and economic life.

So, it is evident that the Muslim pillar of *Turkishness* was flexible enough to include some Jews and Christians, and this was done openly. More problematic, however, has been the inclusion of other larger groups within the population who, while coming within the broad category of Muslim, have not been able to fit comfortably into the Turkish national identity.

The most obvious group in this context is the Kurdish people. I don't intend to get embroiled in a discussion of this issue here, but suffice it to say that, in spite of their Islamic faith, Kurds in Turkey speak an Indo-European language totally unrelated to Ural-Altaic Turkish, and are ethnically quite distinct. Also among the native Muslim population are small communities of Arabic, Laz, Zaza and Romani speakers, not to mention later refugee groups from the Balkan and Caucasus regions, many of whom retain their own languages and cultural traditions.

These communities undoubtedly have issues with the concept of *Turkishness* that presupposes ethnic and linguistic homogeneity, and those issues bind them together within their own groups. There is, however, another significant demographic, numbering, depending on whose estimate you take, somewhere between ten and twenty-five million, or fourteen to thirty-three percent of Turkey's population. These are the people known as *Alevi*, and the huge disparity between the upper and the lower figure perhaps sounds a warning that something mysterious is, or has been going on.

One interesting feature of *Alevism* is that it is to be found in both Turkish and Kurdish communities – it cuts across ethnic and linguistic boundaries. Perhaps that is not so surprising, because Alevism is a religious faith. However, when it comes to describing the characteristics of that faith, the waters become muddy. A word often associated with Alevism is *heterodox* (the opposite of orthodox), meaning that its tenets, beliefs and rituals are difficult to pin down. This is probably because it has never been the established religion of any state or empire. Having no central authority to demand conformity, Alevis have a certain freedom to follow their own tastes and inclinations. On the other hand, another word that recurs in discussions of Alevism is *endogamous*, which means that there is social pressure to marry within the faith. In other words, you and I may have difficulty grasping the concept, but Alevis themselves are quite confident in their own identity.

OK, enough preamble. Let's make some effort to understand what makes them special. Some sources insist that Alevism is a sub-branch of *Shia* Islam - a potential problem in Turkey where the majority follow the state-approved *Sunni* path. Other sources insist, however, that the most important influence is pre-Islamic folk religions such as the shamanism of the original Turkish tribes. It seems, in fact, that both arguments are probably true, which is why some suggest that Alevism is actually the true spirit of Turkish Islam.

If you have been following events in Syria, and making some attempt to understand what's going on there, you have probably heard that one reason Bashar al-Assad doesn't have widespread support is, he belongs to the minority *Alawi* sect. Some sources will tell you that 'Alevi' is the Turkish form of the Arabic 'Alawi' – but beware! There are apparently crucial differences, and Alevism seems to be a peculiarly Turkish phenomenon – this despite the fact that many Kurds adhere.

Confused? Let's take a closer look at those elements outlined above. First up, most of us are aware that there are two main sub-divisions of the Islamic faith: Sunni and Shia. As with the big divisions of Christianity (Eastern Orthodox, Roman Catholic, Protestant), it is easy to see the differences now, in ritual practices and sacred architecture. It is more difficult to understand how the original divergences came about, even for members of the group – and as for explaining to outsiders . . . Try it some time! So it is with the Muslim religion.

When the Prophet, God's messenger Muhammed, died in 632 CE, he unfortunately did not leave instructions as to who would succeed him in the leadership role. Some of his followers believed that it should stay in the family, and opted for Ali, cousin of the late departed and sufficiently esteemed by him to have married Muhammed's daughter. Others, however, held that only a democratic election could produce the most capable leader, and they duly followed that procedure, opting for Muawiyah, a gentleman with some reputation for military prowess.

Without going into too much detail, in 680 there was an event known to history as the Battle of Karbala, when descendants of Muawiyah (led by his son Yazid) defeated and killed Ali's son Hussein and most of his family and supporters. One result was the establishment of the *Umayyad* (Sunni) dynasty, who went on to build an enormous empire covering most of the Middle East, North Africa and into Spain, thereby earning the right to insist on their particular brand of orthodoxy. The Shia group, on the other hand, were effectively disempowered and dispersed, existing happily enough, perhaps, in their own small isolated endogamous communities, developing their own rituals and traditions - until the emergence of the *Safavid* dynasty in Iran in 1501, which controlled an empire that included *'all of modern Iran, Azerbaijan and Armenia, most of Iraq, Georgia, Afghanistan and the Caucasus, as well as parts of Pakistan, Tajikstan, Turkmenistan and Turkey. Safavid Iran was one of the Islamic "gunpowder empires", along with its neighbours, the Ottoman and Mughal empires.*[61] The Safavids, in their wisdom, opted for Shia Islam, thereby establishing that sect's first major power base – and inevitably coming into conflict with their neighbourly brethren in gunpowder, the Ottomans.

Well, we can assume that, as is the nature of state-sponsored religions, Safavid Shi'ism took on characteristics of dogma and orthodoxy. At the same time, as conflict grew between the Iranian Safavids and the Sunni Ottomans, it would be understandable if the Iranians looked for support amongst their Shia brethren within the Ottoman domains. Those brethren, however, as a result of centuries of heterodoxy, had evolved into Alevis. No doubt some of their number would have seen allying themselves with a powerful big brother as a way of escaping orthodox Sunni hegemony. Probably most of them would have been just as happy to get on with their lives without becoming involved in international politics. Unfortunately for the silent majority, the Ottoman Sultan Selim I, known in English as *Selim the Grim*, on his way to the eastern frontier with an army to fight the Safavids, had his minions draw up a list of Shia Alevis (referred

---

61 http://en.wikipedia.org/wiki/Safavid_dynasty

to as *Kizilbash*) of whom 40,000 are said to have been rounded up and slaughtered.

To sum up the Islamic position, then, Alevis are Muslim but not necessarily Turkish (although they live in modern Turkey); Muslim but definitely not Sunni Muslim; of Shia origin but definitely not orthodox Shi'ites. Some characteristics of the Alevi belief system are as follows:

- Freedom of belief and worship. Heterodoxy lies at the core of Alevism. They reject the orthodoxy of rituals and practices enforced by state-sponsored religion. In a sense, Alevis are true democrats – but their free spirits have made them, in the eyes of some, dangerous rebels.

- Following logically from the previous point, Alevis do not accept the requirement to pray five times daily, and do not involve themselves in the culture of the mosque. Grand architecture is not required (cf. *Methodism*) for the communal service of worship known as *cem* (jem) or *cemevi*. Unlike orthodox Islam, services involve music, ritual dance and discussion.

- An eclectic philosophy and system of worship which seem to include elements of folk religion, and even, perhaps, Christianity, Gnosticism and Zoroastrianism. The use of fire, for example, in some rituals, seems evocative of the ancient Persian religion.

- The concept of a spiritual path to be followed, requiring the guidance of a *dede* (teacher or mentor). The path has a sequence of four 'gates' to be passed through, of which the lowest is religious law. In this, Alevism bears the mark of Sufism, *'an inner, mystical dimension of Islam'* which emerged in the 9th and 10th centuries, and was extremely influential in creating the so-called Islamic Golden Age from the 13th to the 16th centuries. In the West we know of Sufism particularly through the writings of the

13th century mystic, Mevlana Jalaladdin Rumi[62]. Alevis tend to follow the path of Rumi's contemporary, Hadji Bektash Veli[63]. There were numerous Sufi sects in Anatolia, but these came under pressure in the later years of the Ottoman Empire, and were finally banned altogether by the Turkish Republic under Mustafa Kemal Atatürk.

Well, I hope I have covered some of the most important aspects here. If you want a detailed explanation of Alevi beliefs and practices, you will need to look elsewhere. My reason for putting finger to keyboard on this particular subject is the appearance of a democratisation package of proposed law reform prepared by the Turkish government. The package apparently contains provisions such as: *'cemevis will be given the status of "beliefs and cultural centers", and in addition, the expenses of cemevis such as electricity and water bills will be covered by the state, while dedes (Alevi religious leaders) will be paid a salary by the state.'* The move is part of a wider programme initiated by Turkey's AK Party government aimed at broadening the scope of democracy in Turkey to include groups such as Kurds and Alevis who have hitherto felt marginalized by the state's insistence on the concept of *Turkishness* discussed earlier.

Undoubtedly, it is time for Turkey to move on from the rigid nationalism that characterized the formative years of the Republic. There are good signs. There is now a more natural acceptance of the place of the Ottoman Empire in Turkish history. It is now possible to utter the words *Kurdish* and *Alevi* in polite conversation without warning fingers being raised to lips and fearful glances directed around the room. The civilian government is in the process of assigning a more conventional role to the nation's armed forces where, one hopes, they will be less likely to stage military takeovers.

Nevertheless, the burden of history and misunderstanding is great. Hard-line Kemalists find it difficult to imagine a world where headscarves

---

62 en.wikipedia.org/wiki/Rumi

63 http://en.wikipedia.org/wiki/Haji_Bektash_Veli

and other symbols of religion are seen outside the mosque, and the army does not step in when the ballot box seems not to have produced a desirable government. Alevis, even more so, have centuries of oppression to exorcise from their minds before they can truly believe that reconciliation means more than enforced assimilation. The 7th century Battle of Karbala still figures in their worldview, as does the 1514 massacre by Selim the Grim – which is why there was such an angry reaction to the proposed name for the new Bosporus Bridge. The recent *Ergenekon* and *Balyoz* trials have suggested that conspirators in the so-called 'deep state' have planned and even carried out violent attacks on prominent Alevi citizens in order to fan the flames of sectarian hatred. Whether or not that is true, there are certainly more recent events, such as the 1993 Sivas hotel fire that contribute to a siege mentality among Alevis. Adding to the mix, the AK Party government of Mr Tayyip Erdoğan is portrayed as representing conservative Sunni Islam – and they themselves undoubtedly contribute to this perception.

Clearly, there is work to be done. Nationalist extremism and sectarian hatred are the enemies of democracy and freedom. Ignorance and fear fuel the fire and unscrupulous seekers of power and wealth fan the flames. The spiritual path of Alevism leads towards the perfect human being, *'defined in practical terms, as one who is in full moral control of his or her hands, tongue and loins (**eline diline beline sahip**); treats all kinds of people equally (**yetmiş iki millete aynı gözle bakar**); and serves the interests of others. One who has achieved this kind of enlightenment is also called **eren** or **munavver**.'*[64]

Not easy to do, but it sounds like a worthy goal.

––

With thanks to Zeynep and Ender for sharing their knowledge. Any errors, however, are my responsibility.

---

64 http://en.wikipedia.org/wiki/Alevi - the words in bold type are Turkish